COPPER Magic!

ONE-POT MEALS

COPPER Magic!

ONE-POT MEALS

NO-FUSS RECIPES FOR THE REVOLUTIONARY NEW NONSTICK COOKWARE

ELLA SANDERS

CASTLE POINT BOOKS
NEW YORK

ISBN 978-1-250-18372-9 (paperback)

Design by Katie Jennings Campbell
Production by Mary Velgos
Photography by Allan Penn or used by permission from Shutterstock.com
Special thanks to Jennifer Calvert.

Our books may be purchased in bulk for promotional, educational, or
business use. Please contact your local bookseller or the Macmillan Corporate
and Premium Sales Department at 1-800-221-7945, extension 5442,
or by e-mail at MacmillanSpecialMarkets@macmillan.com.

First Edition: January 2018

10 9 8 7 6 5 4 3 2 1

Contents

Lunches 33

Dinners 73

Introduction

COPPER COOKWARE is no longer just the stuff of culinary dreams, hanging in picturesque professional kitchens and used for complicated old-world recipes. Not only are today's copper pans attractive but also accessible and technologically advanced—making better cooks of us all! Heat conductive, nonstick surfaces ensure everything cooks evenly and that even the gooiest mess of a meal slips right out of the pan. That means no more burned dinners, no more pans soaking in the sink, and no more agonizing over getting a recipe just right. One-pot meals made in this revolutionary new cookware let you spend less time cooking and cleaning, and more time doing the things you enjoy.

In *Copper Magic! One-Pot Meals*, you'll find more than 75 no-fuss recipes that make the most of your copper pans. Many of these recipes—such as the Glazed Apple Strata, Chicken Corn Chowder, and Ham and Noodle Casserole—cook up beautifully in a deep square copper pan. Recipes such as Shellfish Paella could make good use of an 11-inch copper casserole pan, while the 12-inch pan is perfectly sized for the Blueberry Lemon Skillet Cake, Beef and Broccoli Stir-Fry, and Cajun Chicken Pasta, to name a few favorites.

Each of the recipes in this book was created to give you something easy and delicious to serve up while exploring your copper pans' many advantages. For example, the pans can go straight from the stovetop to the oven for delicious baked dishes and casseroles. And with the copper pans' nonstick surface, oils, butters, and sprays aren't necessary to help a dish easily slide out of the pan every time. Instead, these ingredients are reserved when needed to add flavor or to create the right consistency.

Some recipes make impressive but effortless meals for guests, and others will become family favorites for busy weekdays. Some one-pot meals come together all at once and others in stages, allowing you to start a breakfast recipe, for example, the night before for an easier morning. Make each meal your own by swapping in the ingredients you love and swapping out the ones you (or your family) don't. With copper pans and these simple all-in-one recipes, you don't have to choose between making a great meal for your family and spending quality time with them.

Enjoy!

Breakfasts

Creamy French Toast Casserole

THIS MAKE-AHEAD MEAL IS PERFECT for both casual family breakfasts and guest-filled brunches. Put it in the fridge before bed, and it's ready to go in the oven when you wake up! Dress up the dish by topping it with your favorite fresh fruit, whipped cream, and (of course!) a hefty helping of maple syrup.

SERVES 6–8

1 loaf French or sourdough bread, cubed

4 ounces cream cheese, cubed

8 large eggs

¼ cup sugar

1 teaspoon cinnamon

¼ cup maple syrup

1 teaspoon vanilla

2½ cups milk

4 tablespoon unsalted butter, melted

1   The night before, spread half of the bread cubes into an 11-inch copper casserole pan. Distribute the cream cheese cubes evenly over the top, and layer with the remaining bread cubes.

2   Using a whisk, combine the eggs, sugar, and cinnamon in a large bowl. Then whisk in the maple syrup, vanilla, milk, and melted butter until the ingredients are well combined.

3   Pour the mixture over the bread, and use a spatula to gently press the bread into the liquid to soak. Cover your pan with aluminum foil and store it in the refrigerator for 8–12 hours.

4   In the morning, bake your casserole, uncovered, at 350°F for about 45 minutes, or until the top is golden brown. Serve hot.

Honey Nut Sticky Buns

IF YOUR FAMILY SHARES A SWEET TOOTH, the gooey glaze and caramelized pecans on these breakfast rolls are sure to be a hit. Have company coming over? Just double the recipe and store half of it in a second deep copper pan. This recipe uses pecans, but walnuts or almonds would be an equally scrumptious substitution.

SERVES 9

DOUGH

2 teaspoons active dry yeast	2 tablespoons unsalted butter	1 teaspoon kosher salt
½ cup milk	2 tablespoons granulated sugar	1 large egg
		2 cups all-purpose flour

TOPPING

1 cup packed brown sugar	2 tablespoons unsalted butter	¾ cup chopped pecans
3 tablespoons honey		

FILLING

¼ cup (4 tablespoons) unsalted butter, softened	1 teaspoon ground cinnamon	1 tablespoon all-purpose flour
¼ cup granulated sugar		½ cup raisins (optional)

TO MAKE THE DOUGH

In a large bowl, mix together the yeast, milk, unsalted butter, sugar, salt, egg, and flour. Cover the bowl with plastic wrap, and let rise for 45–60 minutes.

TO MAKE THE TOPPING

In a 10-inch copper pan, heat and stir the brown sugar, honey, and butter until the sugar dissolves. Top with the pecans, remove from the heat, and set the pan aside.

TO MAKE THE FILLING

Combine the softened butter, sugar, cinnamon, and flour in a medium bowl to create a thick spread.

TO ASSEMBLE

1   When the dough has risen, place it onto a floured surface and roll it into a 10 x 12-inch rectangle. Smooth the filling over the dough, and top it off with raisins (optional). From a long side, roll the dough into a log and pinch together the seam. Cut the log into 9 equal rolls.

2   Place the rolls cut-side down into the topping pan, and flatten the rolls until the sides are just slightly touching one another. Cover the pan with plastic wrap and let the dough rise for about 1 hour, or until doubled in size.

3   Bake at 375°F for 30–35 minutes or until deep golden brown. At 15 minutes into baking, tent the top of the pan with foil.

4   Remove the pan from the oven and invert it to empty the rolls onto a large plate. Let the rolls cool for 20 minutes before serving.

Blueberry Lemon Breakfast Cake

THERE'S NO NEED TO WAIT FOR A SPECIAL OCCASION to whip up this cake! Tart lemon zest and yogurt balance out the sweetness of blueberries for a dish that will wake you up with a smile on your face. If blueberries aren't in season, try experimenting with other varieties of fresh fruit.

SERVES 8

1 cup all-purpose flour

½ cup finely ground cornmeal

1 ½ teaspoons baking powder

½ teaspoon kosher salt

½ cup (1 stick) unsalted butter, room temperature

1 cup granulated sugar

2 large eggs, room temperature

½ cup plain yogurt

1 teaspoon vanilla extract

zest of 1 medium lemon, finely grated

1 ½ cups fresh blueberries

powdered sugar, for dusting

1   Preheat the oven to 350°F. In a medium bowl, combine the flour, cornmeal, baking powder, and salt, and set the mixture aside. In a separate bowl, use a hand mixer on a medium-high speed to combine the butter and sugar until light and fluffy.

2   Add the eggs one at a time and beat until the ingredients are well combined. Scrape the mixture down from the sides of the bowl, then add the yogurt, vanilla, and lemon zest. Continue to mix everything until combined, or about 1 minute. (The mixture will look lumpy.) Reduce the mixer to a low speed and slowly add the dry mixture until just combined.

3   Gently fold in the blueberries by hand using a spatula. Pour the batter into a 12-inch copper pan and spread out the batter evenly.

4   Bake the dish for about 30 minutes, or until golden brown around the edges and a toothpick inserted into the center comes out clean. Let the cake cool for at least 20 minutes before topping with powdered sugar. Using a knife, loosen the cake around the edges, slice, and serve.

Chocolate Dutch Baby Pancake

THIS RECIPE IS QUICK, EASY, AND FILLED WITH CHOCOLATE—what more could you ask for? Dutch baby pancakes, or German pancakes, are a light and fluffy twist on an American morning staple. Instead of flipping and frying, just pop your copper pan in the oven for a tasty breakfast before you know it.

SERVES 8

¾ cup whole milk

3 large eggs

⅓ cup all-purpose flour (spooned and leveled)

¼ cup unsweetened cocoa powder, sifted

¼ teaspoon coarse salt

½ teaspoon pure vanilla extract

¼ cup granulated sugar

2 tablespoons unsalted butter

powdered sugar, for dusting

1   Preheat the oven to 425°F. In a blender, add the milk, eggs, flour, cocoa powder, salt, vanilla, and sugar, put on the blender cover, and mix on low until frothy, about 1 minute.

2   In a 10-inch copper pan, melt the butter on a stovetop over medium heat.

Pour the batter evenly into the pan, and immediately place the pan in the oven.

3   Bake for about 20 minutes or until the pancake has risen and set. Top with powdered sugar, and serve.

Dutch Baby Apple Pancake

IF YOU'VE EVER WANTED TO EAT APPLE PIE for breakfast, consider this recipe your free pass. This dish is as pretty as it is mouthwatering, which makes it a great go-to for brunch with guests. And with only 15 minutes of prep time, you'll be able to enjoy both your friends *and* your meal.

SERVES 6

2 tart baking apples, peeled and sliced

7 tablespoons unsalted butter, divided

2 tablespoons sugar

3 large eggs

1 cup milk

¾ cup all-purpose flour

½ teaspoon kosher salt

⅛ teaspoon ground nutmeg

1 teaspoon vanilla

powdered sugar, for dusting

1   In a 10-inch copper pan, add the apples, 4 tablespoons of the butter, and sugar. Cook and stir the ingredients over medium heat until the apples are tender. Transfer the contents to a bowl, and set the bowl aside.

2   Wipe out the pan, then place it in the oven and preheat the oven to 425°F. In a blender, add the eggs, milk, flour, salt, nutmeg, and vanilla, put on the blender cover, and mix on low until smooth.

3   Carefully remove the pan from the oven and add the remaining 3 tablespoons of butter. Bake until the butter bubbles, approximately 1 minute. Remove the pan again and pour in the batter. Bake, uncovered, for 20 minutes or until the pancake rises and the edges are golden brown and crisp. Spoon the apple mixture onto the baked pancake and dust with powdered sugar. Cut and serve immediately.

Apple Cinnamon Whole Grain Breakfast Bake

A HEALTHIER SPIN on the Creamy French Toast Casserole (p. 4), this bake has just the right amount of sweet ingredients to jumpstart your day. You can whip it up the night before and give the wet ingredients time to soak in, or bake it immediately for a slightly less dense consistency. For a smoother texture throughout, remove the bread crusts. (*Note: The recipe calls for 2 pounds of whole grain bread, which is about 2 loaves without the crusts.*)

SERVES 6-8

8 large eggs

2 cups 1% milk, plus 2 tablespoons

⅓ cup dark brown sugar

2½ teaspoons vanilla extract, divided

1½ teaspoons cinnamon, plus extra for dusting

½ teaspoon nutmeg

2 pounds whole-grain bread, sliced ¼-inch thick

3 medium firm apples (about 1¼ pounds), cored and sliced ¼-inch thick

3 ounces cream cheese

2 tablespoons agave syrup

1   The night before, whisk the eggs thoroughly in a medium bowl. Stir in 2 cups of milk, the brown sugar, 2 teaspoons of the vanilla, the cinnamon, and the nutmeg until the ingredients are well combined.

2   In an 11-inch copper casserole pan, create a layer using half of the bread slices. Add a second layer using all of the apple slices. Last, add a third layer with the remaining bread slices. Pour the egg mixture evenly over the top of the layers. Cover with aluminum foil, and refrigerate overnight.

3   When ready to bake, preheat the oven to 350°F. Keeping the foil on, bake the casserole for 45 minutes. (If not making the recipe in advance, reduce the baking time by 10 minutes.) Next, remove the foil, and continue baking for another 15 minutes.

4 Combine the cream cheese, the agave syrup, the remaining 2 tablespoons of milk, and the last ½ teaspoon of the vanilla in a microwave-safe bowl, and warm in the microwave until soft, about 45 seconds. Whisk the ingredients together using a fork, then drizzle the mixture over the top of the warm casserole. Top off the dish with a dusting of cinnamon. Let cool for 10 minutes before serving.

Glazed Apple Strata

THIS MAKE-AHEAD BREAKFAST CASSEROLE is full of the most delightful ingredients—apple pie spice, cinnamon bread, and pecans, to name a few. Prep the ingredients, layer them into your pan the night before, and then bake it when you're ready the next morning.

SERVES 6-8

1 cup packed brown sugar

¼ cup unsalted butter, cubed

2 tablespoons corn syrup

3 large green apples, peeled and chopped

2 tablespoons lemon juice

1 tablespoon sugar

1 teaspoon apple pie spice

1 loaf day-old cinnamon bread

½ cup chopped pecans

10 large eggs

1 cup 2% milk

1 teaspoon kosher salt

1 teaspoon vanilla extract

1½ cups confectioners' sugar, sifted

3 to 4 tablespoons milk

2 teaspoons vanilla extract (optional)

1   Combine the brown sugar, butter, and corn syrup in an 11-inch copper casserole pan to make a caramel sauce. Bring the liquid to a boil over medium heat, stirring continuously. Stir 2 minutes more, or until thickened. Remove the sauce from the pan, and set it aside.

2   In a small bowl, mix together the apples, lemon juice, sugar, and pie spice. Lay half of the bread in the bottom of the pan. Top evenly with the apples and drizzle with the caramel sauce. Evenly distribute a layer of pecans, and top with the remaining bread.

3   Combine the eggs, milk, salt, and vanilla in a large bowl, and pour over the top of the casserole. Press gently using a spatula to ensure the ingredients soak in. Cover with foil and refrigerate overnight.

4   The next morning, bake, uncovered, at 350°F for 50-55 minutes, or until a toothpick comes out clean.

5   While the strata cools, add the confectioner's sugar to a medium bowl and slowly stir in the milk and vanilla, a little at a time, to make a smooth, pourable glaze. Drizzle and serve.

Blueberry Cheesecake French Toast Casserole

NOTHING SAYS BREAKFAST LIKE BAKED BLUEBERRIES! For the perfect French toast casserole consistency, skip soft, fresh bread, which soaks up wet ingredients too easily, resulting in soggy slices. You want the gooey texture in this casserole to come from the cream cheese and baked fruit, and day-old bread provides just the right consistency for a better breakfast balance.

SERVES 6-8

1 loaf French bread, cubed

⅓ cup granulated sugar

1 (8-ounce) package cream cheese

1 teaspoon vanilla extract

1½ cups frozen blueberries

enough all-purpose flour to coat blueberries

8 large eggs

1½ cups milk

1 Layer the bottom of an 11-inch copper casserole pan with half of the cubed bread. In a medium bowl, use a hand mixer to combine the sugar, cream cheese, and vanilla. Distribute the mixture evenly on top of the bread by the teaspoonful.

2 Toss the frozen blueberries in flour, then layer them into the pan. Top the blueberry layer with the remaining bread.

3 In a large bowl, whisk together the eggs and milk, and pour the mixture on top of the bread. Press gently using a spatula to ensure ingredients soak in. Cover with aluminum foil and refrigerate the pan overnight.

4 The next morning, remove the casserole from the refrigerator 30 minutes before baking and preheat the oven to 350°F . Bake the casserole for 45-50 minutes, or until golden brown.

Homestyle Breakfast Hash

THIS SAVORY DISH IS BIG ON PROTEIN AND FLAVOR, making it the perfect start to a busy day. Create a healthier dish by substituting chicken, turkey, or low-sodium bacon for the regular kind. If you're craving something spicier, use Pepper Jack cheese instead of Colby-Jack and top with your favorite hot sauce.

SERVES 6

¼ cup chopped onion

2 teaspoons olive oil

3 slices bacon, diced

1 (20-ounce) package frozen shredded hash browns

½ teaspoon kosher salt

¼ teaspoon freshly ground black pepper

6 large eggs

¾ cup Colby-Jack cheese, shredded

1   Add the onion and olive oil to a 12-inch copper pan and cook over medium heat until translucent. Add the bacon and heat through for about 1 minute.

2   Mix in the hash browns, salt, and pepper. Cook the ingredients over medium heat for 10 minutes or until the hash browns are golden brown on the bottom before flipping them over.

3   Create six nests in the hash browns, and break one egg into each.

4   Cook, covered with a lid, over a low heat for 8–10 minutes, or until the eggs are set and the hash browns are cooked through. Scatter the shredded cheese evenly over the hash, and let the dish stand until melted before serving.

Potato, Pepper, and Parmesan Breakfast Gratin

NO MATTER THE TIME OF DAY, you can't go wrong with potatoes. Add in the sweetness of bell peppers and the bite of Parmesan cheese, and you have yourself a hearty breakfast bake that will wake up your senses. If you like a little meat with your potatoes, top your gratin with a sprinkling of bacon or crumbled sausage (cooked in the same pan before the first step).

SERVES 6-8

2 pounds small red potatoes, sliced ⅛- to ¼-inch thick

1 cup water

1 large red bell pepper, finely diced

4 cloves garlic, minced

1¼ cup Parmesan cheese, grated and divided

10 large eggs

1 cup whole milk

½ cup yogurt

1½ teaspoons kosher salt

freshly ground black pepper

fresh basil or parsley, for garnish

1   Preheat the oven to 350°F. Add the sliced potatoes and water to a large microwave-safe bowl. Cover the bowl and microwave for 5–7 minutes, or until the potatoes are just tender. Drain the potatoes, and lay half of them in the bottom of an 11-inch copper casserole pan.

2   Combine the bell pepper, garlic, and a ½ cup of the Parmesan cheese in a small bowl. Spread the mixture evenly over the potatoes.

3   Whisk together the eggs, then add the milk, yogurt, and a ½ cup of the Parmesan cheese. Season with salt and a liberal helping of black pepper. Pour half of the egg mixture over the potatoes in the pan.

4   Neatly layer on the remaining potatoes. Pour the second half of the egg mixture over the potato layer, and top with the remaining ¼ cup of Parmesan cheese.

5 Bake uncovered for 50–60 minutes, or until the eggs have risen, the gratin is golden around the edges, and a toothpick inserted in center comes out clean.

Let the gratin cool for 5–10 minutes before garnishing with basil or parsley and serving.

Eggs Benedict Casserole

THIS CASSEROLE PROVES you don't have to wait for a fancy breakfast out to indulge in buttery eggs Benedict. Because this recipe takes a little more time to bake, it's better suited to a weekend brunch than breakfast on a busy morning. Make sure you leave yourself enough time (about an hour) for the layers to soak up the egg mixture before putting the whole casserole into the oven. If you notice the top is getting a little too dark while baking, cover the pan with aluminum foil.

SERVES 6

9 tablespoons unsalted butter, divided

8 English muffins, torn into small pieces

1 pound ham steak, chopped

8 large eggs

2 cups whole milk

1 teaspoon garlic powder

kosher salt

freshly ground black pepper

4 large egg yolks

juice of ½ lemon

paprika, for garnish

fresh parsley, torn, for garnish

1   Coat an 11-inch copper casserole pan with 1 tablespoon of the butter, and create layers of torn English muffins and ham, until both of the ingredients are used up.

2   Whisk together the eggs, milk, and garlic powder in a large bowl and season with salt and pepper. Pour the mixture evenly into the pan, and cover with plastic wrap. Refrigerate for 1 hour.

3   When ready to bake, preheat the oven to 375°F. Bake for about 1 hour, or until the eggs are cooked through and the top is golden brown.

4   While the casserole is baking, make a hollandaise sauce by combining egg yolks, lemon juice, and salt in a blender on high for a few seconds. (You can substitute packaged Hollandaise mix if you prefer not to use raw eggs.) With the blender set to low, slowly pour in the remaining 8 tablespoons (one stick) of butter, melted. Put on the blender cover again, and blend on high for about 1 minute. Taste, adding extra lemon and salt as needed.

5   Top the baked casserole with the hollandaise sauce, sprinkle with paprika and parsley, and serve.

Cheesy Ham and Hash Brown Casserole

NOT SURE HOW YOU'RE GOING TO USE THAT LEFTOVER DINNER or holiday ham? This recipe turns a delicious dinner into a hearty breakfast in no time, proving that the best meals don't have to be hard work. Toss just a handful of ingredients together, put the pan in the oven, and enjoy an hour with your family instead of slaving over the stove.

SERVES 8–10

1 (32-ounce) package frozen shredded hash browns

8 ounces ham, cooked and diced

2 (10.75-ounce) cans condensed cream of potato soup

1 (16-ounce) container sour cream

2 cups shredded sharp cheddar cheese

1½ cups grated Parmesan cheese

1   Preheat the oven to 375°F. Combine the hash browns, ham, cream of potato soup, sour cream, and cheddar cheese in a large bowl. Spread the mixture evenly into an 11-inch copper casserole pan, and top the mixture with Parmesan cheese.

2   Bake for about 1 hour, or until the casserole is golden brown and bubbling. Serve immediately.

Sausage and Potato Breakfast Casserole

IF YOU REGULARLY HOST SUNDAY BRUNCH or need a new breakfast find to fill up the kids, this casserole is sure to become one of your favorites. Flavorful, accessible ingredients and a prep time of just 15 minutes make this casserole an easy one to work into your morning roster. Tailor the recipe to your crowd's tastes using mild, sweet, or hot sausage.

SERVES 8

1 pound Italian sausage

1 medium white onion, peeled and diced

1 red bell pepper, diced

3 cloves garlic, minced

1 (20-ounce) bag frozen hash browns, thawed

2 cups cheddar or part-skim mozzarella cheese, shredded and divided

6 large eggs

⅓ cup milk

¼ teaspoon freshly ground black pepper

green onions, thinly sliced for garnish

1   Heat the oven to 375°F. Add the sausage to an 11-inch copper casserole pan, and cook over a medium-high heat, breaking up the meat with a spoon until browned. Using a slotted spoon, transfer sausage to a large mixing bowl. Discard all but 1 tablespoon of the sausage grease.

2   Add the onion and red bell pepper to the remaining grease in the pan. Sauté the ingredients for 5 minutes until cooked. Add the garlic and continue to sauté the mixture for 2 more minutes.

3   Add the pan contents to the bowl with the sausage. Stir in the hash browns and 1½ cups of the cheese. In another bowl, whisk together the eggs, milk, and black pepper, then combine with the hash brown mixture.

4   Pour everything into your copper pan, and top with the remaining ½ cup of shredded cheese. Cover the pan with foil and bake for 20 minutes. Uncover and bake for 10–15 minutes more, or until the potatoes begin to brown. Remove and let stand for 5 minutes. Garnish with green onions before serving.

Cheesy Tater Tot Breakfast Bake

THIS IS ONE OF THOSE GREAT MAKE-AHEAD BREAKFASTS that buys you time in the morning when you need it. And if you don't, just put this dish in the oven as soon as you pull it together. The combination of bacon, sausage, and cheese makes this savory dish almost indulgent, but the energy-packed ingredients are sure to help start your day off right.

SERVES 6-8

4 slices bacon

1 pound ground breakfast sausage, casings removed

2½ cups sharp cheddar cheese, shredded and divided

2 cups whole milk

3 large eggs

½ teaspoon freshly ground black pepper

½ teaspoon onion powder

pinch of kosher salt

2 pounds frozen tater tots

3 tablespoons parsley, chopped, for garnish

1   Fry the bacon in an 11-inch copper casserole pan. Once cooked, let the bacon cool before crumbing and setting it aside.

2   Add the sausage to the pan, and cook over a medium-high heat, breaking up the meat with a spoon until browned. Remove the sausage from the pan. Drain any grease before wiping out the pan and returning the drained sausage to the pan. Evenly distribute 2 cups of the cheese over the sausage.

3   Whisk together the milk, eggs, pepper, onion powder, and salt in a large bowl. Pour the mixture evenly over the cheese and sausage. Arrange the frozen tater tots on top in an even layer. If making ahead, cover the pan tightly with aluminum foil and place in the refrigerator until morning.

4   When ready, preheat the oven to 350°F and bake the casserole on a lower rack for about 35 minutes. Remove the pan from the oven and top with the additional ½ cup of cheese and crumbled bacon. Bake for another 5–10 minutes, or until the sides are bubbling and the top is golden brown. Let the dish stand for 10 minutes, and then garnish with parsley before serving.

Cherry Vanilla Baked Oatmeal

THIS SWEET BREAKFAST BAKE IS NOT ONLY VEGETARIAN but also amazingly flavorful. Cinnamon, almond milk, and nuts combine to create a healthy meal that will keep you energized all morning long. And if you need that energy later in the day, the leftovers also make a yummy snack that travels well.

SERVES 8

1 tablespoon coconut oil or unsalted butter

4 cups fresh or frozen pitted cherries

1½ cups rolled oats

¾ teaspoon ground cinnamon

¾ teaspoon baking powder

½ teaspoon kosher salt

2 large eggs

1½ cups unsweetened almond milk

1 tsp pure vanilla extract

⅓ cup pure maple syrup

¾ cup unsalted hazelnuts

¾ cup unsalted walnuts

1   Preheat the oven to 350°F. Coat a 12-inch copper pan with coconut oil or butter. In the bottom of the pan, add the cherries to create an even layer. Set the pan aside.

2   Combine the oats, cinnamon, baking powder, and salt in a large bowl, and mix until the ingredients are well combined. In a medium bowl, whisk the eggs. Then add the almond milk, vanilla extract, and maple syrup, and continue until the ingredients are well-mixed.

3   Add the contents of the medium bowl to the large bowl, and stir to combine. Pour the mixture evenly over the cherries in the pan. Top the oatmeal mixture with an even layer of hazelnuts and walnuts.

4   Bake the dish for 45 minutes or until the oatmeal is set. Let it stand for 5 minutes before serving.

Raspberry Almond Baked Oatmeal

AFTER YOU MAKE THIS OATMEAL, you'll never go back to instant! Raspberries and almonds pair perfectly to create a healthy breakfast that could easily double as dessert. Plus, this sweet dish is as good the second time around as it is the first, so don't be afraid to store the leftovers in the fridge and reheat them whenever you want a delicious treat.

SERVES 6-8

2 cups old-fashioned rolled oats

⅓ cup brown sugar

1 teaspoon baking powder

½ teaspoon kosher salt

½ teaspoon ground cinnamon

½ cup sliced almonds

2 cups milk or almond milk

1 large egg

3 tablespoons unsalted butter, melted and cooled

¼ teaspoon almond extract

½ cup raspberry jam

Fresh berries, for serving

1   Preheat the oven to 350°F. In a large bowl, combine the rolled oats, brown sugar, baking powder, salt, cinnamon, and almonds. In another bowl, whisk together the milk, egg, butter, and almond extract. Add the wet ingredients to the oat mixture, and stir until the ingredients are well combined.

2   Pour the mixture into a 12-inch copper pan, and spread the raspberry jam over the top. Bake for 30-40 minutes, or until the edges turn golden brown and the mixture is bubbling. Top with fresh berries and serve.

Lunches

Veggie-Filled Sloppy Joes

THIS RECIPE IS PERFECT FOR PICKY EATERS, with flavorful sausage and a hefty helping of veggies hidden in plain sight. Toasting the buns right in the pan sears in the flavor and gives your sandwich a subtle crunch. The recipe calls for pork sausage, but you can use whichever kind you like—choosing to turn up the heat or keep things more mild.

SERVES 4-6

1 pound ground Italian pork sausage

1 cup finely chopped fresh mushrooms

½ cup finely chopped medium onion

½ cup finely chopped green bell pepper

½ cup finely chopped carrots

1 (14.5-ounce) can fire-roasted diced red and yellow tomatoes, undrained

½ cup barbecue sauce

enough butter (salted or unsalted) to spread on buns

4-6 hamburger buns, split

1   In a 12-inch copper pan over medium heat, cook and stir together the sausage (breaking up the meat as you go), mushrooms, onion, bell pepper, and carrots for 8-10 minutes, or until the sausage is browned and the vegetables are tender. Cook the ingredients for another 5 minutes or until most of liquid has evaporated.

2   Add the tomatoes and barbecue sauce, and stir to combine. Bring the liquid to a boil, then reduce the heat and simmer, uncovered, for 15-20 minutes.

3   When the mixture thickens, remove the pan and set aside, taking care to get everything out of the pan. Butter the insides of the buns, and place them cut-side down inside the pan. Fry the buns on low heat until golden brown, about 30 seconds. Spoon the mixture into the buns, and serve.

Beef and Broccoli Stir Fry

THIS SWEET AND SPICY STIR FRY cooks up in just 15 minutes and tastes better than any takeout. For a larger meal, serve it over rice or ramen noodles (just discard the flavor packet). And if you're crazy for spicy food, add as much sriracha as you like—1 teaspoon is merely a suggestion.

SERVES 4

⅔ cup reduced-sodium soy sauce

½ cup chicken stock

¼ cup honey

2 tablespoons rice wine vinegar

¼ cup water

2 tablespoons brown sugar, packed

3 cloves garlic, minced

1 tablespoon sesame oil

1 tablespoon cornstarch

1 teaspoon sriracha

1 teaspoon ground ginger

¼ teaspoon red pepper flakes

1 tablespoon olive oil

1 pound flank steak, sliced thinly across the grain

1 head broccoli, cut into florets

1 Whisk together the soy sauce, chicken stock, honey, vinegar, water, brown sugar, garlic, sesame oil, cornstarch, sriracha, ginger, and red pepper flakes in a medium bowl. Taste the mixture, adding more sriracha if more heat is desired. Set the mixture aside.

2 Heat the olive oil in a 12-inch copper pan over medium-high heat.

Add the steak to the pan and cook for 3-4 minutes, flipping once midway. Cook the steak until browned.

3 Add the broccoli and sauce mixture to the pan, and stir until the broccoli is tender and the sauce is slightly thickened, about 3-4 minutes. Serve immediately.

Chili Con Carne

TAKE YOUR COOKOUT TO THE NEXT LEVEL with this gourmet take on a classic chili dish. Spicy herbs, red wine, and fresh vegetables come together to create a flavor profile your guests will love. For something just a smidge more indulgent, top individual servings with shredded Cheddar cheese. And don't be afraid to tailor the spices to your unique taste.

SERVES 8

2 tablespoons olive oil

1 medium green bell pepper, chopped

2 medium yellow onions, chopped

2 pounds ground beef

1 cup dry red wine

2 (28-ounce) cans diced tomatoes

2 garlic cloves, chopped

1 (12-ounce) can tomato paste

1 teaspoon paprika

2½ teaspoons chili powder

1 teaspoon cayenne pepper

1 teaspoon dried oregano

2 tablespoons fresh parsley, chopped

1 teaspoon kosher salt

1 teaspoon freshly ground black pepper

12 drops hot sauce

2 (15-ounce) cans kidney beans, drained and rinsed

1 (10-ounce) bag frozen sweet corn

1   Heat the oil in a deep square copper pan over medium heat. Add the green bell pepper and onion, and cook until the vegetables are tender. Then add the ground beef, breaking up the meat with a spoon until browned.

2   Stir in the wine, tomatoes, garlic, tomato paste, paprika, chili powder, cayenne pepper, oregano, and parsley.

Season the mixed ingredients with salt and pepper to taste.

3   Bring the liquid to a boil, then reduce the heat, cover the pan with a lid, and simmer for 90 minutes, stirring periodically. Stir in the hot sauce, kidney beans, and corn, and simmer for 30 more minutes before serving.

Chicken Corn Chowder

CHICKEN SOUPS ARE ONE OF THE BEST WAYS to breathe new life into leftovers. No leftovers? No problem! Pick up a rotisserie chicken from your local grocery store and you're already ahead of the game. This recipe is so quick, you can whip it up on your lunch break. For extra flavor, consider adding crumbled bacon or diced roasted red peppers.

SERVES 6

2 tablespoons unsalted butter

¼ cup chopped onion

¼ cup chopped celery

1 jalapeño pepper, seeded and minced

2 tablespoons all-purpose flour

3 cups 2% milk

2 cups roasted and chopped boneless, skinless chicken breasts

1½ cups fresh or frozen corn kernels

1 teaspoon chopped fresh or ¼ teaspoon dried thyme

¼ teaspoon ground red pepper

⅛ teaspoon kosher salt

1 (14.75-ounce) can cream-style corn

1   Melt the butter in a deep square copper pan over medium heat. Add the onion, celery, and jalapeño, cooking and stirring the ingredients until softened, about 3 minutes. Stir the flour into the mixture and cook for 1 additional minute.

2   Add the milk and remaining ingredients, stirring everything to combine. Bring the soup to a boil, and cook until thickened, about 5 minutes.

Chicken Tortilla Soup

CHICKEN TORTILLA SOUP HAS THE MIRACULOUS ABILITY to be both comforting on a cold winter's day and refreshing for a summer lunch break. In this recipe, tart lime juice and cool cilantro balance the heat of the spices and the heft of chicken and black beans.

SERVES 4

1 tablespoon olive oil

½ onion, diced

4 garlic cloves, minced

2 cups chicken broth

1 (10-ounce) can medium enchilada sauce

1 cup crushed tomatoes

1 (15.5-ounce) can black beans, drained and rinsed

1 cup frozen corn

½ teaspoon cumin

¼ teaspoon paprika

¼ teaspoon freshly ground black pepper

2 cups cooked and shredded chicken breasts

1 tablespoon lime juice

1 tablespoon fresh cilantro, chopped, plus extra for garnish

tortilla strips for garnish, if desired

1   Heat the oil in a deep square copper pan over medium heat. Stir in the onion and sauté it for 2–3 minutes. Stir in the garlic, and cook it for 1 minute, or until fragrant.

2   Add the chicken broth, enchilada sauce, crushed tomatoes, black beans, corn, cumin, paprika, and pepper. Lower the heat, and simmer the ingredients for 10 minutes.

3   Stir in the chicken and cook until the meat is warmed through. Remove the pan from the heat, and add the lime juice and cilantro. Garnish with tortilla strips and the remaining cilantro before serving.

Chicken Alfredo

PASTA IS THE ULTIMATE COMFORT FOOD—but all the more so when it's covered in cheesy cream sauce. So when you're having a rough day, why not reach for a lunch of chicken Alfredo instead of the go-to PB and J? This recipe only takes 30 minutes to make and is well worth the extra effort beyond the standard sandwich.

SERVES 4

2 tablespoons extra-virgin olive oil

2 boneless, skinless chicken breasts

kosher salt and freshly ground black pepper

1½ cups whole milk

1½ cups chicken stock

2 cloves garlic, minced

8 ounces fettuccine, uncooked

½ cup heavy cream

1 cup freshly grated Parmesan

fresh basil, for garnish

1   Add the oil to a 12-inch copper pan over medium heat. Season the chicken with salt and pepper, then add the meat to the pan and brown for 8 minutes per side, or until cooked through. Transfer the cooked chicken to a plate and let rest before slicing.

2   Add the milk, chicken stock, and garlic to the pan. Season with salt and pepper, and bring to a simmer. Add the pasta, and cook and stir for about 3 minutes. Let the mixture simmer for 8 more minutes, or until the pasta is as tender as you like.

3   Stir in the cream and Parmesan until the ingredients are well combined. Simmer for 2 more minutes, or until the sauce thickens. Season with more salt and pepper to taste. Remove the pan from the heat, stir in the sliced chicken, and serve the pasta dish with a basil garnish.

Sweet Fire Chicken

WHEN FOOD COURT CRAVINGS call your name, don't answer! Instead, stay home and make this healthier and even-more-delicious alternative. In just 30 minutes, you'll be sitting down to hot pineapple, sweet bell peppers, and spicy chicken so mouthwatering you'll forget all about the mall version.

SERVES 4

1 tablespoon olive oil

1 pound boneless, skinless chicken breasts, cut into 1-inch chunks

1 red bell pepper, chopped

1½ cups diced pineapple, fresh or canned

½ cup Thai sweet chili sauce

2 green onions, thinly sliced

1   Heat the olive oil in a 12-inch copper pan over a medium-high heat.

2   Add the chicken, bell pepper, and pineapple to the pan. Cook for about 3-5 minutes, stirring occasionally, until the bell pepper and pineapple have softened. Stir in the sweet chili sauce until the ingredients are well combined, mixing for about 1–2 minutes. Add more sauce to the dish, if desired, and garnish with green onions before serving.

Quick Pasta Carbonara

BACON, GARLIC, AND PARMESAN CHEESE—oh my! You might balk at pouring raw eggs over your pasta, but the residual heat of the pan and spaghetti will cook them safely. Just don't overdo it, or you'll have pasta tossed with scrambled eggs rather than a rich and creamy Parmesan sauce.

SERVES 4

9 ounces spaghetti, uncooked

1 tablespoon extra-virgin olive oil

6 slices bacon, chopped into ½-inch pieces

2 cloves garlic, minced

2 large eggs

¾ cup grated Parmesan, plus extra for serving

kosher salt and freshly ground black pepper

1 tablespoon chopped parsley, for garnish

1 In a deep square copper pan, cook the pasta in boiling water according to the package instructions. Drain the spaghetti from the pan, toss it with olive oil, and set the pasta aside.

2 Cook the bacon over medium heat, until the pieces are brown and crisp. Stir in the garlic and cook it for one minute, or until fragrant. Add the pasta back to the pan, and toss to coat in the bacon fat. Remove the pan from the heat.

3 Using a fork, beat together the eggs and Parmesan cheese in a small bowl. Pour the mixture into the pan, and toss it with the bacon and spaghetti. Season with salt and pepper to taste, and garnish with extra Parmesan cheese and parsley to serve.

Garlic Butter Shrimp Pasta

JUST THE WORDS GARLIC, BUTTER, AND PASTA are enough to make your mouth water, but add shrimp and Parmesan to the mix and you may have the perfect lunch. As easy to make as it is delicious, this dish is sure to make it into your regular midday meal rotation. Craving more greens? Toss in some baby spinach leaves when you combine the pasta, shrimp, and sauce.

SERVES 4

12 ounces fettuccine, uncooked

4 tablespoon unsalted butter, divided

1 pound shrimp

kosher salt and freshly ground black pepper

4 cloves garlic, minced

¾ cup dry white wine

juice of ½ lemon

pinch of crushed red pepper flakes

¾ cup grated Parmesan, plus more for serving

1 tablespoon freshly chopped parsley

1 In a deep square copper pan, cook the pasta in boiling water according to the package instructions. Drain the fettuccine from the pan, and set it aside.

2 In the same pan, melt 1 tablespoon of the butter over medium heat. Add the shrimp, and season generously with salt and pepper. Cook until the shrimp are pink and opaque, about 2 minutes per side. Remove the shrimp from the pan, and set them aside.

3 Add the remaining 3 tablespoons of butter and the garlic to the pan. Cook until aromatic, about 1 minute. Stir in the wine, lemon juice, and crushed red pepper flakes, and simmer for 2 minutes. Last, stir in the Parmesan cheese and parsley, and simmer for an additional 2 minutes.

4 Add the cooked pasta and shrimp back to the pan, and toss with the garlic butter mixture until the ingredients are well combined. Top the dish with more Parmesan cheese, to taste, before serving.

Crustless Ham and Cheese Quiche

AS PERFECT FOR SUNDAY BRUNCH as it is for a weekday lunch, this creamy quiche is both hearty and satisfying. If you like a little bit of bite, add 4 chopped green onions when you sauté the ham. Using a deep square copper pan for the entire recipe ensures you'll only have one piece of cookware to clean up at the end of the meal rather than two saucepans and a baking dish.

SERVES 8

½ pound cooked ham, diced

1⅔ cups water

1 cup whipping cream

2 garlic cloves, pressed

2 tablespoons unsalted butter

1 teaspoon kosher salt

¼ teaspoon freshly ground black pepper

⅔ cup uncooked quick-cooking grits

1¼ cups shredded Swiss cheese, divided

8 large eggs, divided

½ cup milk

basil, for garnish

1   Preheat the oven to 350°F. In your deep square copper pan, sauté the ham over medium-high heat for 5 minutes. Remove the ham from the pan, and set it aside.

2   Add the next 6 ingredients to the pan, and bring the combined ingredients to a boil. Slowly stir in the grits. Reduce the cooking heat, cover the pan with a lid, and simmer everything for 5–7 minutes, stirring occasionally. Stir in a ½ cup of the cheese until melted,

then remove the pan from the heat, and let stand for 10 minutes. In a small bowl, lightly beat 2 eggs, and stir them into the grits mixture.

3   Level the mixture in the pan using a spatula, and bake, uncovered, for 20 minutes. Then remove the pan from oven and increase the oven temperature to 400°F.

4   While the oven temperature rises, spread the ham mixture evenly over the baked grits. In a medium bowl, whisk together the milk and the remaining 6 eggs before pouring atop the ham. Top with an even layer of the remaining ¾ cup of cheese.

5   With the oven temperature increased, transfer the pan back to the oven, and bake for 35 minutes. Let the dish stand for 10 minutes before cutting and garnishing with basil (if desired) to serve.

Pizza Rigatoni Bake

HAVE A LITTLE FUN WITH FRIDAY LUNCH by combining two family favorites: pizza and pasta. Eight servings go fast when everyone wants seconds! While you're welcome to make your marinara sauce from scratch, using your favorite store-bought brand keeps things quick for an easy meal.

SERVES 8

16 ounces ground Italian sausage

½ cup pepperoni, divided with ¼ cup cut into strips

1 23-ounce jar marinara sauce

3 cups water

1 (16-ounce) box rigatoni pasta

2 cups part-skim shredded mozzarella cheese

kosher salt and freshly ground black pepper

1   Preheat the oven to broil. In an 11-inch copper casserole pan, cook the sausage, breaking up the meat with a spoon until browned. Drain any excess fat before adding the pepperoni strips to the pan. Cook for an additional 1 minute.

2   Stir in the marinara sauce, and season it with salt and pepper to taste. Add the water and pasta, stir the ingredients together, and bring the liquid to a boil. Reduce the heat, cover the pan with a lid, and simmer until the pasta is cooked through and tender, about 15 minutes.

3   Remove the pan from the heat, and top evenly with the mozzarella cheese and the remaining half of the pepperoni (kept in whole slices). Transfer the pan to oven, and broil for about 2 minutes or until the cheese is melted and golden brown. Serve warm.

Honey Lime Shrimp

SOMETIMES THE SIMPLEST DISHES ARE THE MOST FLAVORFUL. This recipe has fewer than 300 calories, so it's a great meal when you're looking for healthier options. The good news is with all of these fresh and filling ingredients, you're sure to walk away from the table feeling satisfied.

SERVES 4

2 tablespoons olive oil, divided

1 pound raw shrimp, peeled and deveined

kosher salt and freshly ground black pepper

¼ cup honey

2 teaspoons garlic, minced and divided

juice of 1 lime

1 pound asparagus, sliced

1 red bell pepper, sliced

1 Heat 1 tablespoon of the oil in a 12-inch copper pan over medium-high heat. Add the shrimp to the pan, and season it with salt and pepper to taste. Stir in the honey, 1 teaspoon of the garlic, and the lime juice until the ingredients are combined. Cook everything for about 4 minutes, flipping the shrimp 2 minutes in. When the shrimp are pink and opaque, remove them from the pan and set aside.

2 Wipe out your pan, and place it over medium heat. Heat the remaining 1 tablespoon of oil, then add the asparagus, bell pepper, and remaining garlic to the pan. Season everything with salt and pepper, and toss the ingredients to combine. When the vegetables are tender, add the shrimp back to the pan and toss again. Serve warm.

Deep Dish Pepperoni Pizza

One of the best things about pizza is that it's almost impossible to encounter a flavor fail. Deep Dish Pepperoni Pizza lets the pepperoni take the lead, with just the right amount of veggies to come in for support. The best part is, you can mix and match with whatever you have in your fridge if green peppers or mushrooms aren't your thing.

SERVES 4

1 tablespoon olive oil

2 tablespoons unsalted butter

1 tablespoon roasted garlic, chopped

1 (16-ounce) package refrigerated pizza dough

cup part-skim mozzarella cheese, shredded and divided

½ cup pizza sauce

2 ounces pepperoni slices

6-8 grape tomatoes, halved

½ green pepper, seeded and sliced

½ cup sliced cremini mushrooms

Italian seasoning, to taste

Parmesan cheese, grated, to taste

Fresh basil, for garnish

1 Preheat the oven to 450°F.

2 Add the butter and garlic to the pan and set the heat to low. Once the butter is melted, coat the entire pan and remove it from the heat. Spread the dough evenly into the pan, carefully pushing the edges up the sides 1-1½ inches. Let the dough rest for a few minutes.

3 Layer ½ of the mozzarella cheese evenly onto the dough. Make another layer using the sauce, and then the remaining mozzarella cheese. Layer the pepperoni, grape tomatoes, green peppers, and mushrooms on top. Finish the dish off with a topping of Italian seasonings and Parmesan cheese, to taste.

4 Bake the pizza for 25-30 minutes, or until the crust is golden brown and the cheese and sauce are bubbling. Let the dish stand for 5-10 minutes before cutting and serving.

Chili Mac and Cheese

TALK ABOUT COMFORT FOOD! The creaminess of the cheese pairs perfectly with flavorful chili spices in this combination of two American classics. In just 30 minutes, you'll have a hearty lunch that everyone—even the little ones—can appreciate. And with copper cookware, this cheesy chili will slide right out of the pan.

SERVES 4

1 tablespoon olive oil

2 cloves garlic, minced

1 onion, diced

8 ounces ground beef

4 cups chicken broth

1 (14.5-ounce) can diced tomatoes

¾ cup canned white kidney beans, drained and rinsed

¾ cup canned kidney beans, drained and rinsed

2 teaspoons chili powder

1½ teaspoons cumin

kosher salt, to taste

freshly ground black pepper, to taste

10 ounces elbow macaroni, uncooked

¾ cup shredded Cheddar cheese

2 tablespoons chopped fresh parsley leaves, for garnish (optional)

1   Heat the oil in a deep square copper pan over a medium-high heat. Add the garlic, onion, and ground beef, breaking up the meat with a spoon until browned, about 3–5 minutes. Drain any fat from the pan.

2   Add the chicken broth, tomatoes, beans, chili powder, and cumin, and stir together. Season the mixture with salt and pepper, to taste. Stir in the pasta, and bring the liquid to a boil. Then, cover the pan with a lid, reduce the heat, and simmer the ingredients for 13–15 minutes, or until the pasta has cooked.

3   Remove the pan from the heat. Top evenly with cheese, and cover with a lid until melted. Garnish the dish with parsley before serving.

Turkey Chili

THIS TURKEY CHILI PACKS A FLAVOR-FILLED PUNCH with garlic, spices, and hot sauce. Using turkey in place of beef is a simple way to lower the amount of saturated fat and calories while avoiding potential heart health risks associated with consuming red meat. This kind of protein swap doesn't work in every recipe, but turkey happens to be a perfect flavor complement to a hearty chili.

SERVES 5

1 tablespoon olive oil

1 cup chopped sweet onions

1 tablespoon minced garlic

¼ cup chopped yellow bell peppers

3 medium zucchini, halved lengthwise and sliced

1 pound ground turkey

1 (28-ounce) can crushed organic tomatoes, undrained

1 (16-ounce) can red kidney beans, drained and rinsed

1 tablespoon chili powder

1 tablespoon sugar

2 cups low-sodium chicken stock

½ teaspoon garlic powder

1 teaspoon hot sauce

1½ teaspoons kosher salt

1 teaspoon dried basil

½ teaspoon dried oregano

green onions, chopped, for garnish

1 Add the olive oil, onions, garlic, bell peppers, and zucchini to a deep square copper pan, and sauté the ingredients over medium heat until the onion is translucent. Stir in the ground turkey, breaking up the meat with a spoon until browned.

2 Stir in the remaining ingredients until everything is well combined. Reduce the heat and let the dish simmer for 1 hour, uncovered, stirring every so often. Garnish with green onions, and serve.

Cheesy Turkey and Rice

PEOPLE ARE BEGINNING TO DISCOVER the wonders of ground turkey. It can be used as a healthy alternative to ground beef in recipes like meatloaf, chili, or burgers—or in a delicious dish all its own (like this one!). Cheesy turkey and rice is a comfort food that whips up quickly for an easy family lunch.

SERVES 6

1½ cups uncooked brown rice

1 pound lean ground turkey

2 cups chopped onion

2 cloves garlic, minced

1 (10.75-ounce) can cream of mushroom soup

1 (4-ounce) can chopped green chiles

½ cup chicken broth

1 cup shredded Cheddar cheese, divided

corn or tortilla chips, crushed, for garnish

chopped cilantro, for garnish

1   Cook rice according to package directions in a 12-inch copper pan. When the rice is tender, remove from the pan and set aside.

2   Place the same pan over medium-high heat, and crumble the ground turkey into the pan. Stir in the chopped onion and garlic, and cook the ingredients together until the turkey has browned and onion has softened.

3   Stir in the cooked rice, soup, chiles, and broth, and cook until heated through. Stir in ¾ cup of cheese, reserving ¼ cup for the topping. Serve the dish topped with extra cheese, crushed chips, and cilantro.

Shrimp Fried Rice

SKIP THE RESTAURANT, AND MAKE THIS HEALTHIER FRIED RICE
at home. Green bell peppers and sriracha add hints of sweet and spice for a recipe
that tops typically bland takeout. Can't get enough veggies? Add in broccoli florets
and mushrooms while you sauté your carrots and peppers.

SERVES 4

1½ cups uncooked
white rice

1 tablespoon vegetable oil

2 cloves garlic, minced

2 carrots, peeled and
finely chopped

1 green bell pepper, finely
chopped

1 pound shrimp, peeled
and deveined

1 cups peas, defrosted

2 tablespoons soy sauce

2 teaspoons sesame oil

1 large egg, whisked

2 tablespoons sliced green
onions

sriracha, to taste

1   Cook rice according to package
directions in a 12-inch copper pan. When
the rice is tender, remove from the pan
and set aside.

2   Add the oil to the same pan over
medium heat. Add the garlic and stir for
1 minute until fragrant. Next, stir in the
carrots and bell pepper, and sauté the
ingredients for 3 minutes. Last, add the
shrimp and cook for 2 minutes on each
side, or until just pink and opaque.

3   Add and stir in the cooked rice, peas,
soy sauce, and sesame oil, and cook for
2 more minutes.

4   Push the rice mixture to one side of
the pan, and pour the egg onto the other.
Stir the egg constantly until mostly
scrambled, then fold the cooked egg
into rice.

5   Top the dish with sriracha sauce and
green onions, and serve.

Sausage and Pepper Frittata

THE NONSTICK SURFACE OF YOUR COPPER PAN takes the frustration out of creating amazing egg dishes like a frittata, which is a hearty one-pan meal simpler to make than it looks. While this recipe is a delicious way to start your day, savory sausage and cheese also make a great combo for lunch or dinner.

SERVES 8

12 large eggs

kosher salt and freshly ground black pepper

¼ cup grated Parmesan or Romano cheese

½ cup grated Cheddar or Monterey Jack cheese

enough olive oil to coat pan

½ pound sweet Italian sausage, casings removed

2 tablespoons unsalted butter

1 medium onion, halved and sliced thin

2 bell peppers, sliced thin

2 cups baby spinach leaves

1   Preheat the oven to 375°F. Beat the eggs in a bowl, then season them lightly with salt and pepper. Mix in the grated cheeses and set aside.

2   Add the olive oil to coat a 12-inch copper pan over medium-high heat. Add the sausage to the pan, breaking up the meat with a spoon until browned, about 6–8 minutes. Use a slotted spoon to transfer the sausage to a plate. Drain the fat from the pan and set the sausage aside.

3   Melt the butter over medium-high heat. To the pan, add the peppers and onions, and sauté the ingredients until soft and browned. Add the spinach and cook for 1 minute. Return the sausage to the pan.

4   Distribute the veggies and meat in an even layer across the bottom of the pan before pouring in the egg and cheese mixture. Cook over medium-high heat for 30–45 seconds to set the edges, then transfer the pan to the oven.

5   Bake for 10–12 minutes. Remove the pan once the eggs are set and before the top browns. Serve immediately.

Deep Dish Veggie Pizza

IF YOU'RE A VEGGIE LOVER, THIS PIZZA IS FOR YOU. In this recipe, you get to pick your favorites, such as mushrooms, bell peppers, eggplant, cherry tomatoes, and onions (to name a few). Using packaged pizza dough saves you time so that you can make this delicious deep dish without spending half your day to do so.

SERVES 4

1 tablespoon olive oil

1 cup mixed vegetables (based on personal preference)

2 tablespoons unsalted butter

1 tablespoon roasted garlic, chopped

1 (16-ounce) package refrigerated pizza dough

½ cup part-skim mozzarella cheese, shredded and divided

½ cup pizza sauce

Italian seasoning, to taste

Parmesan cheese, grated, to taste

fresh basil, for garnish

1   Preheat the oven to 450°F. Add the oil to a deep square copper pan over medium-high heat. Add the vegetables to the pan, stirring to coat with the oil. Sauté and stir the vegetables until they are tender-crisp. Remove the vegetables from the pan, and set them aside.

2   Add the butter and garlic to the pan and reduce the heat to low. Once the butter is melted, coat the entire pan and remove it from the heat. Spread the dough evenly into the pan, carefully pushing the edges up the sides 1–1½ inches. Let the dough rest for a few minutes.

3   Layer ½ of the mozzarella cheese evenly onto the dough. Make another layer using the vegetables, then the sauce, and then the remaining mozzarella cheese. Finish the dish off with a topping of Italian seasonings and Parmesan cheese, to taste.

4   Bake the pizza for 25–30 minutes, or until the crust is golden brown and the cheese and sauce are bubbling. Let the dish stand for 5–10 minutes before cutting and serving.

Loaded Baked Potato Soup

LOADED BAKED POTATO SOUP HAS ALL THE HALLMARKS of comfort food: bacon, ham, cheese, potatoes, and milk. This recipe makes 15 cups, so you'll have enough soup for both seconds *and* leftovers—and it's so tasty you'll want both! Although creamy soups don't freeze well, this dish will keep in the fridge for several days (although those 15 cups may not last that long).

SERVES 15 —————————————————————————————

⅔ cup unsalted butter

¾ cup all-purpose flour

4 cups milk, divided

12 ounces bacon

1½ cups chopped onion

6 cups chicken broth

2 pounds baking potatoes, peeled and cubed

1 teaspoon kosher salt

1 teaspoon freshly ground black pepper

1 cup cooked ham

8 ounces sour cream

2½ cups shredded sharp Cheddar cheese, divided

¾ cup sliced green onions, divided

1   In a deep square copper pan, melt the butter over low heat. Add the flour to the pan, and whisk until smooth, then cook and stir for 1 minute more. Slowly stir in 2 cups of the milk. Remove the mixture from the pan and set it aside. Wipe out the pan.

2   Turn up the heat to a medium setting, add the bacon, and cook it until crisp, about 6–7 minutes. Once cooked, place the bacon onto paper towels to absorb the grease as it cools. Crumble the bacon, and set it aside. Drain all but 2 tablespoons of bacon drippings from the pan.

3   Turn up the heat to a medium-high setting, and cook the onion in the pan drippings until they are almost tender. Add the broth and potatoes, and bring the liquid to a boil. Reduce the heat to low, and cook the ingredients for 10 minutes, or until the potatoes are soft.

4   Add the flour-and-milk mixture to the pan. Stir in the remaining 2 cups of milk, and season with the salt and

pepper. Increase the heat to a medium setting, and whisk continuously until the mixture is thick and bubbling.

5 Stir in the ham, half of the bacon, the sour cream, 2 cups of the cheese, and a ½ cup of the green onions. Cook until thoroughly heated and cheese has melted. Divide into servings and top evenly with the remaining bacon, cheese, and green onions.

Broccoli Mac and Cheese

MAC AND CHEESE IS ONE OF LIFE'S GREATEST PLEASURES. But pair it with broccoli and cheddar, and you've got yourself a go-to meal. While elbow macaroni may be the first pasta that springs to mind, you can use whatever kind of pasta strikes your fancy in the moment.

SERVES 4

2 cups heavy cream

2½ cups water

2 tablespoons unsalted butter

1 tablespoon prepared yellow mustard

½ teaspoon kosher salt

½ teaspoon freshly ground black pepper

2 cups dry pasta

1 (12-ounce) package frozen broccoli

2½ cups shredded sharp Cheddar cheese

1 In a deep square copper pan, stir together the heavy cream, water, butter, mustard, salt, and pepper. Bring the liquid to a boil over a medium-high heat.

2 Stir in the pasta, and reduce the heat to a medium-low setting. Simmer the ingredients for 7–10 minutes, stirring regularly.

3 Add the frozen broccoli, and let everything cook (stirring frequently) until the pasta is as firm as you like and the broccoli is heated through. Add the shredded cheese, and stir until it is completely melted. Season with an additional dash of salt and pepper to taste, before serving.

Vegetable Frittata

BRIGHT VEGETABLES, PROTEIN-PACKED EGGS, and superfood spinach combine to make a lunch that won't leave you lagging. This dish takes little effort but looks gourmet, making it a great option to serve to guests.

SERVES 4

8 large eggs

⅓ cup milk

½ teaspoon kosher salt

¼ teaspoon freshly ground black pepper

2 tablespoons olive oil

1 medium red bell pepper, thinly sliced

2 medium zucchini, halved lengthwise and thinly sliced

½ small onion, thinly sliced (about ½ cup)

2 cups packed baby spinach

4 ounces feta cheese

1   Preheat the oven to 350°F. Beat together the eggs, milk, salt, and pepper in a large bowl.

2   Add the oil to a 10-inch copper pan over medium heat. Stir in the red pepper, zucchini, and onion, and sauté the ingredients until softened, about 7 minutes. Add the spinach and cook it until wilted, about 2 minutes.

3   Layer the vegetables evenly in the pan, and top with the egg mixture.

Crumble feta cheese over the top of the eggs and cook 2–3 minutes without stirring, or until the eggs are just beginning to set around the edges.

4   Transfer the pan to the oven, placing it on the middle rack. Bake for 15 minutes, or until the frittata is almost set in center. Change the oven setting to broil, and cook the frittata until the top is golden brown, about 2 more minutes. Remove the pan from the oven, and let the dish stand for 5 minutes before serving.

Dinners

Beef Stroganoff

SKIP THE PROCESSED, BOXED VERSION, and go straight for this healthier and more gratifying grown-up version of beef Stroganoff. This recipe uses ground beef and mimics the dish your family already loves. And thanks to the nonstick surface of your copper pan, cleaning up those creamy noodles will be a breeze. To take this dish the the extra mile, sauté thinly sliced sirloin tips in place of the ground beef.

SERVES 4-6

1 tablespoon olive oil

8 ounces cremini mushrooms, stems trimmed and sliced ¼-inch thick

½ teaspoons kosher salt, plus more to taste

½ teaspoon freshly ground black pepper, plus more to taste

2 tablespoons unsalted butter

1 medium yellow onion, finely diced

2 medium garlic cloves, finely chopped

1 pound ground beef

3 tablespoons all-purpose flour

1 teaspoon paprika

¼ cup dry white wine

4 cups low-sodium beef broth or stock

8 ounces dry egg noodles

¾ cup sour cream

1   Add the oil to a deep square copper pan over medium-high heat, and add the mushrooms. Season them with salt and pepper, and brown them for about 5 minutes, stirring occasionally. Remove the mushrooms from the pan, and set them aside in a medium bowl.

2   Reduce the heat to a medium setting, and add the butter. Once the butter is melted, stir in the onion and garlic, season the ingredients with salt and pepper, and cook everything for 4-5 minutes, or until softened.

3   Add the beef to the pan and season with salt and pepper, breaking up the meat with a spoon until browned, about 6–8 minutes, stirring occasionally. Drain off any excess fat.

4   Sprinkle in the flour and paprika and stir together with the meat to coat it. Continue cooking the ingredients for 1–2 minutes, stirring occasionally. Add the wine and cook for 1–2 minutes, occasionally scraping the bottom of the pan until the wine has reduced. Last, stir in the broth, measured salt, and measured pepper until all ingredients are well combined. Increase the heat to a medium high setting.

5   Add the noodles and cooked mushrooms (including the juices) to the pan, and stir everything together to combine. Reduce the heat, and simmer for 6–8 minutes, stirring occasionally until the noodles are just cooked through.

6   Remove the pan from the heat, and stir in the sour cream. Season the dish with salt and pepper as needed, and serve.

Hearty Beef Stew

YOU DON'T NEED TO USE A COLD SNAP or rough day as an excuse to make this rich stew. Mustard and red wine add a little bit of bite to an otherwise traditional dish, giving you a reason to reach for this recipe over and over again.

SERVES 4

1½ pounds beef chuck roast, trimmed and cut into ¾-inch cubes

1 teaspoon freshly ground black pepper

1½ teaspoons kosher salt, divided

1 tablespoon canola oil

3 medium carrots, cut into 1-inch pieces

1 medium yellow onion, cut into 12 wedges

6 cloves garlic, chopped

1 cup dry red wine

2 tablespoons all-purpose flour

4 cups beef broth, divided

12 ounces new potatoes, cut into chunks

2 tablespoons whole-grain mustard

1 tablespoon red wine vinegar

1   Season the beef with the pepper and 1 teaspoon of the salt. Add the oil to a deep square copper pan over medium-high heat. Stir in the beef, and cook for about 6 minutes, stirring the meat occasionally until brown on all sides. Transfer the beef to a plate, and set it aside.

2   Add the carrots and onions to the pan, and cook for 4–6 minutes, stirring frequently, until the vegetables start to soften. Add the garlic, and cook for 1 additional minute, stirring occasionally. Stir the in red wine, and cook 10-12 minutes, or until the liquid has reduced, occasionally scraping the bottom of the pan to combine the ingredients.

3   In a small bowl, whisk together the flour and a ½ cup of the broth before adding the mixture to the pan. Stir in the cooked beef, the remaining ½ teaspoon of salt, and the remaining 3½ cups of broth. Bring the liquid to a boil.

4   Reduce the heat to a medium-low setting, cover the pan with a lid, and let the dish simmer for 45 minutes. Stir in the potatoes, cover the pan again, and cook until softened, about 20 minutes. Finish by stirring in the mustard and vinegar before serving hot.

Classic Beef Pot Roast

THE WARMTH AND COMFORT OF POT ROAST fill you from head to toe, so it's just right for chilly days. But it's also a great any-day dinner when conversations, cheering up family members, and savoring time together is what the meal is most meant for. Just make sure to leave yourself time to cook the beef to full tenderness.

SERVES 10

1 teaspoon olive oil

1 (3-pound) boneless chuck roast, trimmed

1 teaspoon kosher salt

¼ teaspoon freshly ground black pepper

2 cups coarsely chopped onion

1 cup dry red wine

4 thyme sprigs, plus extra for garnish (optional)

3 garlic cloves, chopped

1 (14-ounce) can fat-free, low-sodium beef broth

1 bay leaf

4 large carrots, peeled and cut diagonally into 1-inch pieces

2 pounds Yukon gold potatoes, peeled and cut into 2-inch pieces

1   Preheat the oven to 350°F. In a deep square copper pot, add the oil over medium-high heat. Season the chuck roast with the salt and pepper. Add the roast to the pan and cook for 5 minutes, browning all sides of the roast. Remove the roast from the pan and set it aside.

2   Add the onion to the pan, and sauté it for 8 minutes, or until softened. Return the browned roast to the pan, and add the red wine, thyme, garlic, beef broth, and bay leaf to the pan. Cover the pan with a lid, transfer it to the oven, and bake the roast for 1½ hours, or until it is almost tender.

3   Remove the pan from oven, and add the carrots and potatoes. Cover the pan again and bake the roast for an additional 1 hour or until the vegetables are tender.

4   Remove the pan from the oven, and discard the thyme and bay leaf. Shred the roast using two forks to pull the tender meat apart. Serve the roast and the vegetables in a bit of the cooking liquid, garnishing with fresh thyme, if desired.

Italian Style Pot Pie

GROUND ROUND, SAUSAGE, AND MUSHROOMS fill up this Italian twist on a classic meat pie. If you're looking for more greenery, serve it with a side salad or bake in a few of your favorite veggies. Eggplant, tomatoes, or bell peppers would all complement this dish beautifully.

SERVES 4–6

¾ pound ground round

¼ pound mild Italian sausage, casings removed

1 small onion, chopped

2 garlic cloves, minced

8 ounces fresh mushrooms, sliced

26 ounces tomato-and-basil pasta sauce

½ teaspoon dried Italian seasoning

¼ teaspoon kosher salt

1 (13.8-ounce) package refrigerated pizza crust

Enough all-purpose flour to roll out the dough

1 cup shredded Italian five-cheese blend

1   Preheat the oven to 450°F. Cook and stir the beef and sausage in a deep square copper pan over medium-high heat for 8–10 minutes, or until browned and crumbly. Remove the meat from the pan and set it aside. Drain off any excess fat, reserving 1 teaspoon of drippings in the pan. Reduce the heat to a medium setting.

2   Add the onion to the hot pan drippings, and sauté for 2 minutes. Stir in the garlic, and cook for 1 minute. Add the mushrooms, and sauté them for 8–10 minutes, or until most of liquid has reduced. Stir in the beef-sausage mixture, the pasta sauce, the Italian seasoning, and the salt. Bring the liquid to a boil, then reduce it to a simmer for 5 minutes.

3   While the pie contents cook, unroll the dough on a lightly floured surface, and cut it to fit over your square pan with a ½ inch to spare on each side.

4   Sprinkle cheese over the beef mixture. Top the pan with the cut dough, and seal the dough over the edges using your fingers (being very careful not to burn yourself!). Slice a small "X" into the center of the dough to allow steam to escape while baking.

5   Bake the pie for 16–20 minutes, or until the crust is golden brown. Let it rest for 10 minutes before serving.

Short Rib Stew

THIS RECIPE TAKES STEW TO THE NEXT LEVEL. Short ribs turn mouthwateringly tender when simmered at length, and ingredients like red wine and cremini mushrooms add to the richness of this dish. The heat-conductive surface of your copper pan ensures that every ingredient cooks perfectly.

SERVES 8

3½ pounds boneless beef short ribs, cut into 1½-inch pieces

¼ cup all-purpose flour

3 tablespoons extra-virgin olive oil

2 cups dry red wine

3 cups chicken stock

6 carrots, cut into ½-inch pieces

1½ pounds Yukon Gold potatoes, peeled and cut into ½-inch pieces

3 medium parsnips, peeled and cut into ½-inch pieces

1 large onion, cut into 1-inch pieces

½ pound cremini mushrooms, quartered

1 tablespoon chopped fresh thyme leaves

8 sage leaves, coarsely chopped

kosher salt, to taste

freshly ground black pepper, to taste

1   In a large bowl, toss together the short ribs and flour. Add the oil to a deep square copper pan over medium-high heat. Working in batches, cook the short ribs until browned on all sides, about 6 minutes per batch. Discard the oil from the pan.

2   Return the meat and any juices to the pan. Add the wine, and boil until reduced by half, about 8 minutes. Add the stock, cover the pan with a lid, reduce the heat, and simmer the meat until it's tender, about 2 hours.

3   Skim off any fat from the stew and discard. Stir in the carrots, potatoes, parsnips, onion, mushrooms, thyme, and sage. Cover the pan with the lid, and simmer for about 35 minutes, or until the vegetables are tender. Season with salt and pepper, to taste, and serve.

Macaroni and Cheeseburger

YOU CAN MAKE MACARONI AND CHEESE a million different ways, but turning it into a combination of cheeseburgers and creamy pasta might just be one of the best. If you're feeling guilty about a lack of vegetables, sauté diced tomatoes with your ground beef for a healthy and flavorful addition.

SERVES 4

1 pound elbow macaroni, uncooked

kosher salt, to taste

1 pound ground beef

freshly ground black pepper, to taste

1 clove garlic, minced

1 cup crushed tomatoes

1 cup whole milk

2 cups shredded Cheddar cheese, divided

parsley, for garnish

1   In a deep square copper pan, cook the pasta according to the package directions until al dente, seasoning the water generously with salt. Drain and set aside.

2   In the same pan over medium-high heat, add the ground beef, breaking up the meat with a spoon until browned. Season with the salt and pepper, add the garlic, and cook for 1 minute more. Drain off any excess fat. Add the tomatoes and milk, and bring the liquid to a boil before reducing the heat and simmering for 5 minutes.

3   With the heat on a low setting, stir in the pasta, and add 1 cup of the cheese a little at a time. Stir the ingredients until they are well combined before adding more cheese. Top with the remaining cheese, cover the pan with a lid, and simmer until the cheese is melted and bubbling, about 1 minute. Garnish with parsley before serving.

Chicken Pot Pie

THIS SIMPLE POT-PIE-IN-A-PAN brings you all of the savory scrumptiousness of the traditional dish with none of the fuss. Cooking and baking in one pan keeps everything moving along quickly—including cleanup, which is especially easy with a copper pan. Chicken pot pie freezes beautifully, so don't be afraid to box up the leftovers.

SERVES 4-6

1 tablespoon olive oil

1½ pounds boneless, skinless chicken breasts, cubed

2 teaspoons kosher salt, divided

1 teaspoon freshly ground black pepper, divided

½ white onion, chopped

2 cloves garlic, minced

1 cup Yukon Gold potatoes, cubed

2 cups frozen peas and carrots

4 tablespoons unsalted butter

4 tablespoons all-purpose flour

2 cups chicken broth

1 teaspoon kosher salt

½ teaspoon freshly ground black pepper

1 (14.1-ounce) packaged pie crust, thawed if frozen

egg wash (1 large egg mixed with 2 tablespoons water)

1 Preheat the oven to 400°F. Add the oil to a 12-inch copper pan over medium heat. Add the cubed chicken, season with 1 teaspoon of the salt and ½ teaspoon of the pepper, and cook the meat until no longer pink. Remove the chicken from the pan, and set it aside.

2 Return the pan to the medium heat setting, and add onions and garlic. Sauté the ingredients until translucent. Stir in the potatoes and cook for about 5 minutes. Stir in the peas and carrots, and cook for an additional 1 minute. Add the butter to the vegetables, and stir the ingredients until the butter is melted.

3 Add the flour to the pan, stirring quickly to coat the vegetables and avoid any lumps. Pour in the chicken broth, bring the liquid to a boil, and cook the ingredients until the sauce thickens. Season with the remaining salt and pepper, stir in the cooked chicken, and remove the pan from the heat.

4 Lay the pie dough over the top of the pan, and seal the edges using your fingers (being very careful not to burn yourself!). Slice a small "X" into the center of dough to allow steam to escape. Brush the dough the with egg wash. Bake for 25–30 minutes or until golden brown, and serve hot.

Shepherd's Pie

SIMPLE AND SATISFYING, this version of shepherd's pie uses packaged ingredients and beef instead of lamb to speed up the kitchen time. Remember, there's no shame in shortcuts! As for the vegetables, peas and carrots are traditional, but feel free to mix up things with whatever you and your family like best.

SERVES 6

1 package instant mashed potatoes

4 ounces cream cheese, cubed

1 cup shredded Cheddar cheese, divided

2 garlic cloves, minced

1 pound ground beef

4 cups frozen mixed vegetables, thawed

1 cup beef gravy

1 Preheat the oven to 375°F. Prepare the mashed potatoes according to the directions and set 2 cups of them aside in a large bowl. Add the cream cheese, ½ cup of the shredded cheese, and the garlic to the potatoes and mix until the ingredients are well combined.

2 Brown the meat in a deep square copper pan, and drain off any excess fat. Stir the vegetables and gravy into the beef. Top evenly with the potato mixture.

3 Top with a sprinkling of the remaining ½ cup of cheese. Bake for 20 minutes, or until heated through, and serve immediately.

Chili and Biscuit Bake

TALK ABOUT COMFORT FOOD! BUTTERY BISCUITS bake right on top of robust chili for a dinner that takes less than an hour to put on the table. Have an overzealous oven? Cover the top of the pan with foil if the biscuits start to get too dark too quickly.

SERVES 4–6

1 tablespoon extra-virgin olive oil

1 onion, chopped

2 cloves garlic, minced

1 pound ground beef

1 cup kidney beans, drained

1 tablespoon cumin

1 tablespoon paprika

kosher salt and freshly ground black pepper

1 (15-ounce) can fire-roasted tomatoes

1 (8-ounce) can tomato sauce

1 (7.5-ounce) can refrigerated biscuit dough

¼ cup unsalted butter, melted

½ teaspoon garlic powder

1 teaspoon chopped parsley

1   Preheat the oven to 375°F. Add the oil to a 12-inch copper pan over medium heat. Add the onion, and sauté it until tender, about 5 minutes. Stir in the garlic, and cook it until fragrant, about 1 minute more. Add the ground beef, breaking it up with a spoon until browned, about 5 minutes. Remove the meat mixture from the pan and set it aside. Drain off any excess fat.

2   Return the pan to a medium heat setting and add the kidney beans, cumin, and paprika, and season the ingredients with salt and pepper, to taste. Stir in the tomatoes and tomato sauce, reduce the heat, and simmer the ingredients for 5–10 minutes.

3   While the pan contents are simmering, prepare the biscuit topping. Cut each biscuit in half, and roll each half into a ball. In a small bowl, whisk together butter, garlic powder, and parsley until well combined. Submerge each dough ball in the butter mixture, then place evenly over the top of chili.

4   Place the pan in oven, and bake until the biscuits are golden brown, about 30 minutes. Let the dish cool for 10 minutes before serving.

Honey Garlic Chicken and Veggies

THIS EASY WEEKNIGHT DINNER IS A NO-BRAINER. A simple glaze of lemon juice, olive oil, honey, and garlic turns basic chicken and veggies into something wonderful. And using a copper pan ensures everything cooks perfectly. Although chicken thighs tend to be juicier and more flavorful, you could easily swap in boneless, skinless chicken breasts.

SERVES 2–3

⅓ cup lemon juice

2 tablespoons olive oil, plus extra to drizzle

3 tablespoons honey

1 clove garlic, minced

1 tablespoon butter

1 pound boneless, skinless chicken thighs

kosher salt and freshly ground black pepper

8 ounces green beans, trimmed

8 ounces cherry tomatoes

2 carrots, sliced

1 Preheat the oven to 400°F. In a small bowl, whisk together the lemon juice, olive oil, honey, and garlic. Set the mixture aside.

2 Heat butter in a 12-inch copper pan. Season the chicken with salt and pepper, then add it to the pan and brown it for 2–3 minutes on each side. Remove the meat from the pan, momentarily setting it aside.

3 Evenly distribute the green beans, cherry tomatoes, and carrots in the same pan. Return the chicken to the pan, placing the chicken thighs on top of vegetables. Pour the lemon mixture over the top of the pan contents.

4 Transfer the pan to the oven, and bake for 15–20 minutes, or until the chicken is cooked through (the internal temperature of the chicken should reach 165°F). Serve the chicken with a helping of vegetables, and top each serving with sauce from pan.

Cilantro Lime Chicken and Rice

CRAVING A BURRITO BOWL? Save money and skip the line by cooking your own at home. This tasty combination of chicken, vegetables, and rice serves six and cooks up in no time, filling your home with the aroma of citrus and spices. If, by some miracle, you don't finish it off the first time, just heat up any leftovers on the stove in your copper pan for equally delicious seconds.

SERVES 6

1 teaspoon + 1 tablespoon olive oil, divided

1 pound boneless, skinless chicken breast, cubed

½ teaspoon kosher salt, plus more to taste

¼ teaspoon freshly ground black pepper, plus more to taste

1 small yellow onion, diced

2 poblano peppers, chopped

2 cloves garlic, minced

2½ cups low-sodium chicken broth

juice of 1 lime

1 (14.5-ounce) can cooked black beans, drained

1 (15.25-ounce) can of corn

2 tomatoes, diced

1½ cups uncooked jasmine rice, rinsed

3 tablespoons chopped cilantro

1   Add 1 teaspoon of the olive oil in 12-inch copper pan over medium-high heat. Add the chicken to the pan, and season with salt and pepper, to taste. Cook the chicken until no longer pink, about 6–8 minutes. Remove the chicken from the pan, and set it aside.

2   Heat the remaining 1 tablespoon of olive oil in the same pan. Stir in the onion and peppers, and sauté them for 5–7 minutes. Add the garlic, and cook for 1 additional minute.

3   Stir in the chicken broth, lime juice, black beans, corn, tomatoes, rice, measured salt, and measured pepper to combine all of the ingredients. Reduce the heat, cover the pan with a lid, and simmer the ingredients for 15-20 minutes, or until the rice is cooked through. Stir in the cooked chicken and cilantro and serve.

Shrimp and Asparagus Bowties

Simple and delicious, Shrimp and Asparagus Bowties are an easy way to get a well-rounded meal on the table. Crunchy asparagus and healthy shrimp go especially well together, and the grape tomatoes add a nice burst of flavor. This doesn't even need a sauce—the Parmesan coats the pasta for a perfect cheesy finish!

SERVES 6

1 tablespoon olive oil

1 pound asparagus, stalks cut in half and ends removed

½ teaspoon garlic powder

kosher salt and freshly ground black pepper

8 ounces farfalle, uncooked

2 cups water

1 pound shrimp, peeled and deveined

1 cup halved grape tomatoes

½ cup Parmesan cheese

fresh parsley, for garnish

1   Add the olive oil to a deep copper square pan over medium heat. Add the asparagus, tomatoes, and garlic powder and sauté for 1-2 minutes. Season the mixture with salt and pepper, to taste.

2   Reduce the heat to a simmer, and stir in the uncooked pasta and water. Bring the liquid to a boil before reducing the heat, covering the pan with a lid, and simmering until the pasta is cooked to your preference, about 13–15 minutes.

3   Remove the lid and add the shrimp and grape tomatoes, stirring occasionally. Cook for 3-4 minutes, or until the shrimp is red.

4   Remove the pan from the heat and stir in the Parmesan cheese until it is well combined. Garnish the dish with parsley and serve immediately.

Creamy Lemon Chicken and Potatoes

WHEN TART LEMON COMBINES WITH LUSCIOUS CREAM, you know you're in for a treat! Fresh chicken and a hearty serving of vegetables round out this delicious and deceptively easy dish. If you use traditional green beans instead of *haricot verts*, just make sure you steam them before adding them to the pan.

SERVES 4

12 ounces baby red potatoes, halved

enough water to cover the potatoes

3 teaspoons olive oil, divided

4 (6-ounce) skinless, boneless chicken breast halves

¾ teaspoon kosher salt, divided

½ teaspoon freshly ground black pepper, divided

2 thyme sprigs

4 ounces cremini mushrooms, quartered

1 tablespoon chopped fresh thyme

¼ cup whole milk

5 teaspoons all-purpose flour

1¾ cups unsalted chicken stock

8 thin lemon slices

8 ounces trimmed *haricots verts* (French green beans)

parsley, chopped, for garnish

1   Preheat the oven to 450°F. Add the potatoes to a 12-inch copper pan, and cover with water. Bring the liquid to a boil, before reducing the heat and simmering for 12 minutes, or until the potatoes are tender. Drain the water, remove the potatoes from the pan, and set aside.

2   Return the pan to the stovetop, and add 1 teaspoon of the oil to the pan over medium-high heat. Pound the chicken to a ¾-inch thickness, and sprinkle with ¼ teaspoon each of the salt and pepper. Add the chicken and thyme sprigs to the pan, and cook for 5 minutes to brown the chicken. Turn the chicken over, transfer the pan to oven, and bake for 10 minutes

or until the chicken is cooked through. Remove the chicken from the pan and set it aside.

3   Return the pan to a medium-high heat, and cook the remaining 2 teaspoons of oil. Add the potatoes (cut-side down), mushrooms, and chopped thyme, and cook for 3 minutes or until the potatoes are browned after stirring once.

4   In a small bowl, whisk together the milk and flour. To the pan, add the remaining salt, the remaining pepper, the milk-and-flour mixture, the chicken stock, the lemon slices, and the beans. Simmer for 1 minute or until the sauce thickens slightly. Return the chicken to the pan, cover with a lid, reduce the heat, and simmer the ingredients for 3 minutes, or until the beans are tender-crisp. Garnish the meal with parsley before serving.

Sweet and Sour Chicken

SKIP THE TAKEOUT MENU and make this satisfying sweet-and-sour chicken dish at home in no time. Sweet pineapple and bell peppers balance out a tangy hint of heat for a taste you'll love almost as much as you'll appreciate how easily the sticky sauce slips mess free from your copper pan. If you're craving more veggies, add some broccoli and carrots to the mix. Serve it on its own or over rice or noodles.

SERVES 4

1 tablespoon vegetable oil

¾ pound boneless chicken, cubed

1 cup green and red bell pepper, cut into strips

1 tablespoon cornstarch

¼ cup light soy sauce

1 (8-ounce) can pineapple chunks in juice

3 tablespoons vinegar

3 tablespoons brown sugar

½ teaspoon ground ginger

½ teaspoon garlic powder

1   Add the oil to a 12-inch copper pan, then cook and stir the chicken until it is well-browned. Stir in the peppers, and cook for 1 to 2 minutes.

2   Mix in the cornstarch and soy sauce. Add the pineapple and its juice, vinegar, sugar, ginger, and garlic powder. Bring the liquid to a boil until the sauce thickens. Serve while hot.

Easy Chicken Chow Mein

IN LESS TIME THAN IT TAKES TO PICK UP FOOD from your favorite Asian restaurant, you can pull together this delicious and healthy dish in a single pan. Looking for a little extra color and vitamin C? Slice up a red bell pepper and cook it with the peas and carrots. Don't have egg noodles on hand? A box of whole-grain spaghetti works just as well!

SERVES 5-6

1 tablespoon canola oil

2 boneless, skinless chicken breasts, cubed

1 cup stringless snap peas, sliced thin

1½ cups shredded cabbage or coleslaw mix

1 large carrot, peeled and shredded

1 teaspoon minced garlic

½ teaspoon minced ginger

1-2 pinches red pepper flakes

4 cups chicken broth

½ cup soy sauce

¼ cup hoisin sauce

1 (16-ounce) package dry egg noodles

1 Heat the oil in a deep square copper pan. Add the chicken, and cook over medium-high heat until mostly browned. Add the peas, cabbage, and carrot, and cook for 2-3 minutes, until the vegetables are tender.

2 Add the garlic, ginger, and pepper flakes to the pan, and cook everything for 1 minute. Stir in the broth, soy sauce, and hoisin sauce, and bring the liquid to a boil. Add the pasta before reducing the heat to a medium setting.

3 Cook and stir the pasta for 5 minutes, until the pasta is separated and most of the liquid has been absorbed. Cover the pan with a lid, and cook for an additional 3-4 minutes, until the pasta is cooked to your liking. Serve immediately.

Spicy Chicken and Black Bean Enchiladas

THIS FAMILY FAVORITE IS SURE TO SPICE UP any weeknight without adding too much to your to-do list. If you're running low on time, use a store-bought rotisserie chicken instead of cooking your own. Looking to lighten things up? Swap in low-fat cheese and fat-free sour cream for the full-fat versions used here.

SERVES 4

¼ cup chicken broth

1 (16-ounce) skinless, boneless chicken breast

1 medium onion, diced

1 red bell pepper, diced

1 (15-ounce) can black beans, drained and rinsed

1 cup whole-kernel corn

¼ cup chopped and packed fresh cilantro

1 (4-ounce) can diced green chiles

2¼ cups shredded sharp Cheddar cheese

⅔ cup fat-free sour cream

hot pepper sauce

kosher salt and freshly ground black pepper

8 (6-inch) flour tortillas

⅔ cup enchilada sauce

1   Preheat the oven to 350°F. Bring the chicken broth to a simmer in a 12-inch copper pan. Add the chicken breast to the broth, cover the pan with the lid, and simmer the meat until cooked through (about 25 minutes), turning once in the liquid. Remove the chicken from the pan and let cool, before shredding and setting aside in a large bowl. Discard any remaining chicken broth.

2   In the same pan, add the onions and red bell pepper. Sauté over medium heat until soft, about 5 minutes.

3   Transfer the cooked onions and peppers to the bowl of chicken, and add the beans, corn, cilantro, chiles, 2 cups of the cheese, and sour cream. Mix until the ingredients are blended, adding the hot sauce, salt, and pepper to taste.

4   Divide the mixture evenly into the centers of the tortillas, rolling and lining them up in the copper pan, seam-side down. Pour the enchilada sauce over top of the tortillas and finish with the rest of the cheese. Bake for 35 minutes, or until the sauce begins to bubble and the enchiladas are cooked through.

Cajun Chicken Pasta

CREAMY MONTEREY JACK CHEESE AND CRISP BELL PEPPER balance out the heat from Cajun spices in this multifaceted pasta dish. If you're a red sauce kind of person, chop up some cherry tomatoes and cook them with the pepper and onion to bring in the tomato flavor you're seeking.

SERVES 4-6

1 tablespoon olive oil

1¼ pounds boneless, skinless chicken thighs, cut into chunks

kosher salt and freshly ground black pepper

2 tablespoons Cajun seasoning, divided

1 red bell pepper, diced

½ large onion, diced

2 cloves garlic, minced

2 cups chicken broth

10 ounces farfalle, uncooked

2 tablespoons heavy cream

1½ cups Monterey Jack cheese, shredded

parsley for garnish

1   Add the oil to a 12-inch copper pan over medium-high heat, and add the chicken. Season the meat with salt, pepper and 1 tablespoon of the Cajun seasoning. Cook the chicken until browned on all sides, stirring occasionally. Stir in the bell pepper, onion, and garlic, and cook for 2-3 minutes more, or until the vegetables are tender.

2   Stir in the chicken broth and the uncooked pasta. Bring the liquid to a gentle boil, then reduce the heat, cover the pan with a lid, and simmer the ingredients for 10-15 minutes or until the pasta is tender, stirring every so often.

3   Set the oven to broil. To the pan, add the heavy cream and the remaining Cajun seasoning, and stir until combined. Top evenly with the cheese, transfer the pan to the oven, and broil the dish for 2-3 minutes, or until the cheese melts and begins to brown and bubble. Remove the pan from oven, letting it cool slightly before garnishing with parsley and serving.

Penne alla Vodka with Shrimp

BUTTERY MARINARA-AND-CREAM SAUCE and Parmesan cheese are the ultimate indulgence. For an equally satisfying vegetarian spin, simply omit the shrimp. Or make it even richer by using prosciutto instead: Just sauté ⅛ pound prosciutto in place of the shrimp. Any which way you dish it up, it's sure to be amazing!

SERVES 6

1 pound pasta, uncooked

1½ teaspoons + 2 table-spoons olive oil, divided

12 ounces medium shrimp, peeled and deveined

3 tablespoons unsalted butter, divided

½ medium onion, chopped finely

2 cloves garlic, chopped

½ cup vodka

1 (14-ounce) can tomato puree

1 cup heavy cream

1 pinch red pepper flakes

¼ teaspoon kosher salt

freshly ground black pepper, to taste

1 cup grated Parmesan cheese, divided

1 small tomato, sliced into wedges

1   In a deep square copper pan, cook the pasta according to the package directions. Drain the pasta and set it aside.

2   In the same pan, add 1½ teaspoons of the oil over medium-high heat. Add the shrimp, and sauté them for 2 minutes on each side, or until they are opaque and no longer pink. Remove the shrimp from the pan, and set them aside with the pasta.

3   Add the remaining 2 tablespoons of olive oil and 2 tablespoons of butter to the pan. When the butter has melted, stir in the onion and garlic, and cook for 2 minutes. Pour in the vodka, then stir and cook for 3 more minutes. Stir in the tomato puree, before reducing the heat to a simmer, stirring in the cream, and seasoning with red pepper flakes, salt, and pepper, to taste. Stir in the last tablespoon of butter until melted.

4   Add the cooked pasta and shrimp to the sauce, tossing all of the ingredients to combine. Stir in ¾ cup of the Parmesan cheese until melted. Divide the pasta into servings, topping evenly with the remaining Parmesan cheese and serving hot. Top with tomato wedges as a final touch.

Broccoli Cheddar Chicken and Rice Casserole

PICKY EATERS WILL DELIGHT in this simple and scrumptious cheesy casserole, and you'll be thrilled you only have one pan to clean up. From start to finish, the whole process takes just 40 minutes, making this a great go-to dinner for busy weeknights. Don't be afraid to add a bit more chicken broth if the rice requires it.

SERVES 6

1 tablespoon olive oil

1 small onion, chopped

2 chicken breasts, cubed

kosher salt and freshly ground black pepper

4 cloves garlic, minced

¾ cup white rice, uncooked

1 (10-ounce) can cream of chicken soup

2–3 cups chicken broth

2 cups broccoli florets

1 cup shredded Cheddar cheese, divided

1 tablespoon chopped fresh parsley, for garnish

1   Add the olive oil to a 12-inch copper pan over medium heat. Add the onion and chicken, and cook until the chicken starts to brown, about 3–4 minutes. Season the ingredients with salt and pepper to taste. Stir in the garlic, and cook everything for another 30 seconds, or until the garlic is fragrant.

2   Add the rice, cream of chicken soup, and chicken broth to the pan. Bring the liquid to a boil, before reducing the heat to a medium setting and cooking for about 15 minutes. Stir the dish occasionally, until the rice is fully cooked. Add more salt and pepper for taste if needed.

3   Set the oven to broil. Stir in the broccoli florets and half of the cheese, and cook for 2 minutes more, or until the broccoli is tender. Top evenly with the remaining cheese, and transfer the pan to the oven to broil for 2 minutes, or until the cheese melts and begins to brown and bubble. Garnish the dish with parsley before serving.

Easy Stovetop Lasagna

WHY LABOR OVER LASAGNA WHEN YOU DON'T HAVE TO? This easy stovetop version tastes just as wonderful but is done in just 30 minutes! And by using a copper pan instead of a baking dish, you'll save yourself all that scraping and soaking during cleanup.

SERVES 6

1 tablespoon olive oil

3 Italian sausage links, casings removed

1 (14.5-ounce) can diced tomatoes

1 (8-ounce) can tomato sauce

1 teaspoon dried oregano

1 teaspoon dried basil

½ teaspoon garlic powder

½ teaspoon crushed red pepper flakes

kosher salt and freshly ground black pepper

8 ounces farfalle, uncooked

2 cups water

1 cup part-skim shredded mozzarella cheese

¼ cup freshly grated Parmesan cheese

1 cup ricotta cheese

fresh basil, for garnish

1 Add the olive oil to a 12-inch copper pan over medium-high heat. Add the Italian sausage, breaking up the meat with a spoon until browned, about 3–5 minutes. Drain off any excess fat.

2 Stir in the diced tomatoes, tomato sauce, oregano, dried basil, garlic powder, and red pepper flakes. Season the mixture with salt and pepper, to taste.

3 Reduce the heat to a simmer, and stir in the uncooked pasta and water. Bring the liquid to a boil before reducing the heat, covering the pan with a lid, and simmering until the pasta is cooked to your preference, about 13–15 minutes.

4 Remove the pan from the heat, and stir in the mozzarella and Parmesan cheeses until the ingredients are well combined. Top with dollops of ricotta, and cover the pan with a lid until heated through, about 2–4 minutes. Garnish the dish with basil, and serve immediately.

Pesto Chicken Pasta

IF YOU'RE CRAZY ABOUT NUTS, this pesto pasta recipe is for you. Walnuts, pecans, and whole wheat pasta combine with chicken and sun-dried tomatoes to create a hearty aroma and flavor. For extra added greens, mix in 3 ounces of spinach just before you finish cooking.

SERVES 4

1 clove garlic, minced

4 ounces fresh basil, roughly chopped

½ teaspoon kosher salt, divided plus extra to taste

¼ teaspoon freshly ground black pepper, plus extra to taste

2 tablespoons walnuts

3 ounces olive oil + 1 tablespoon olive oil, divided

4 tablespoons fresh grated Parmesan cheese

1 pound boneless, skinless chicken breast tenders

3 cloves garlic

2 cups low-sodium chicken broth

4 ounces sun-dried tomatoes, drained

8 ounces whole wheat pasta, uncooked

¼ teaspoon red pepper flakes

green onions, chopped, for garnish

pecans, for garnish

TO MAKE THE PESTO SAUCE

In a food processor, add the garlic, basil, ¼ teaspoon of the salt, measured pepper, and walnuts. While blending, slowly pour in the 3 ounces of olive oil. Puree thoroughly before adding in the Parmesan and pulsing to mix. Set the pesto aside.

TO ASSEMBLE

1 Add the remaining 1 tablespoon of olive oil to a deep square copper pan on medium-high heat. Season the chicken with salt and pepper to taste, and brown the meat on both sides. Cook the chicken thoroughly for 8–10 minutes, before removing from the pan and setting aside.

2 Sauté the garlic in the pan for 1–2 minutes, or until fragrant. Stir in the chicken broth, sun-dried tomatoes, pasta, remaining ½ teaspoon of salt, and red pepper flakes until combined. Cover the pan with a lid, and bring the liquid to a boil. Reduce the heat, and simmer for 10–15 minutes, or until the pasta is cooked to your preference. Pour in the pesto, and stir everything together to combine. Top the pasta with green onions and pecans, if desired, and serve.

Ham and Noodle Casserole

PUT LEFTOVER HAM TO GOOD USE with your new favorite recipe. Cheesy, creamy, and oh-so-tasty, this casserole is sure to make the whole family happy. Serve the dish with a salad, or sneak in another veggie, such spinach or red bell pepper, before cooking.

SERVES 4

8 ounces pasta, uncooked

2 tablespoons unsalted butter, divided

1½ cups cooked ham, chopped

1 cup shredded Cheddar cheese

1 cup frozen peas

1 (10½-ounce) can cream of chicken soup

½ cup low-fat milk

1 Preheat the oven to 375°F. In an 11-inch copper casserole pan, cook the pasta according to the package directions. Drain the pasta and briefly set aside. Coat the pan with 1 tablespoon of the butter, and then add half of the pasta back to the pan.

2 In a small bowl, combine the ham, cheese, and peas. In another small bowl, combine the soup and milk. In the bottom of the pan, evenly layer half of the ham mixture. Top with half of the soup mixture, then the remaining noodles. On top of the noodles, layer the remaining ham mixture and the remaining soup mixture.

3 Top the casserole with evenly distributed dollops of the remaining 1 tablespoon of butter. Cover the pan loosely with foil, and bake for 30 minutes. Let stand for a few minutes, then serve.

Tomato-Basil Pasta

YOU WON'T FIND A PASTA RECIPE EASIER THAN THIS ONE! Throw everything into one deep copper pan, and it cooks all at once, allowing you to put dinner on the table in just 30 minutes without any fuss. If you're looking for a larger serving of veggies, add a sliced red bell pepper with your tomatoes and onion, and stir in baby spinach with your basil.

SERVES 4

12 ounces pasta, uncooked

1 (15-ounce) can diced tomatoes with liquid

1 medium sweet onion, cut in ¼-inch strips

4 cloves garlic, thinly sliced

4½ cups full-sodium vegetable broth

¼ teaspoon red pepper flakes

2 teaspoons dried oregano leaves

2 tablespoons extra virgin olive oil

kosher salt and freshly ground black pepper

1 bunch (10-12 leaves) basil, diced, plus additional leaves for garnish

Parmesan cheese for garnish

1   Add the pasta, tomatoes, onion, and garlic to an 11-inch copper casserole pan. Pour in the vegetable broth, and season the mixture with the pepper flakes and oregano. Drizzle the olive oil over the top.

2   Cover the pan with a lid, bring the liquid to a boil before reducing the heat and simmering for about 10 minutes,

stirring occasionally. Cook until the liquid has reduced almost entirely.

3   Season the dish with salt and pepper, to taste. Stir in the diced basil leaves and toss the pasta to thoroughly combine with the little remaining liquid in the pan. Top the pasta with Parmesan cheese and extra basil before serving.

Cheesy Lemon Chicken Pasta

SHARP PARMESAN AND CREAMY MOZZARELLA complement the brightness of lemon is this creamy pasta dish. Sneaking superfood kale into this cheesy mix ensures that picky eaters won't revolt. And because you're using a copper pan, the cheese won't cause a problem when it's time to clean up.

SERVES 4

2 tablespoons olive oil

½ cup diced yellow onion

1 pound chicken breast, diced

kosher salt and freshly ground black pepper

1 tablespoon minced garlic

10 ounces pasta, uncooked

2 cups chicken broth

¼ cup water

3 heaping cups baby kale

4 ounces cream cheese

½ cup part-skim shredded mozzarella cheese

¼ cup grated Parmesan cheese

3 tablespoons lemon juice, freshly squeezed

sliced lemon, for garnish

1   Add the olive oil to a 12-inch copper pan over medium heat. Add the onions and stir the ingredients until soft, about 3 minutes. Add the chicken to the pan, season it with salt and pepper, and cook the meat until brown on both sides. Add the garlic, and cook everything for one additional minute, or until fragrant.

2   Stir in the uncooked pasta, chicken broth, water, and baby kale, and bring the liquid to a boil. Reduce the heat, cover the pan with a lid, and simmer the dish for 22 minutes. Uncover and cook until the liquid is reduced almost entirely, about 5 minutes.

3   Remove the pan from the heat, and stir in the cream cheese, mozzarella, Parmesan, lemon juice, and sliced lemon, until the cheese is melted. Serve hot.

Creamy Zucchini Mushroom Pasta

BREAK OUT THIS NO-FUSS RECIPE when you have absolutely no time to cook but can't eat another drive-thru hamburger. A light and tasty Parmesan-cream sauce adds a little luxury while mushrooms and zucchini keep things balanced. Boost the veggie quotient by throwing in some peas with the pasta and stirring in baby spinach at the end.

SERVES 6

1 pound spaghetti, uncooked

1 pound cremini mushrooms, thinly sliced

2 zucchini, thinly sliced and quartered

2 cloves garlic, thinly sliced

2 sprigs thyme

4½ cups water

kosher salt and freshly ground black pepper

⅓ cup Parmesan cheese, grated, plus additional for serving

¼ cup heavy cream

1 In a deep square copper pan over medium-high heat, combine all of ingredients except the Parmesan cheese and heavy cream. Season the mixture with salt and pepper, to taste.

2 Bring the liquid to a boil, then reduce the heat, and simmer, uncovered, until the pasta is cooked through and the liquid has reduced, about 8–10 minutes. Stir in the Parmesan cheese and heavy cream. Top the pasta with an additional dusting of Parmesan, and serve immediately.

Caramel Apple Pork Chops

PORK CHOPS AND APPLES ARE A MATCH made in recipe heaven! If you prefer your greens cooked in apple-cinnamon glaze to being in a bowl with dressing (and who wouldn't?), add 12 ounces of fresh baby spinach to your pan for the last couple minutes of simmering. Whether you use bone-in or boneless chops is entirely up to you, though bone-in ones tend to be more flavorful.

SERVES 4

4 strips bacon

4 (6-ounce) pork chops

¼ kosher salt, plus extra

¼ teaspoon freshly ground black pepper, plus extra to taste

3 small tart apples, peeled and diced

1 medium onion, chopped

4 teaspoons brown sugar

1 tablespoon unsalted butter

¼ teaspoon ground cinnamon

½ cup chicken broth

3 tablespoons chopped walnuts, toasted

1 Cook the bacon in a 12-inch copper pan over medium heat until crisp. Remove the bacon and let it cool on paper towels before chopping and setting aside. Drain the grease from the pan, reserving 3 teaspoons of drippings in a small bowl.

2 Return 2 of the 3 teaspoons of drippings to the pan, add the pork chops, and season with salt and pepper. Cook the pork over medium heat for 2–3 minutes on each side, or until lightly browned. Remove the meat from the pan and keep it warm.

3 In the same pan, sauté the apples and onion in the remaining 1 teaspoon of reserved drippings until the apples are tender-crisp. Stir in the brown sugar, butter, measured salt, cinnamon, and measured pepper. Add the broth, and bring the liquid to a boil. Return the pork chops to the pan, reduce the heat, and cover the pan with a lid. Simmer for 4–5 minutes, or until a thermometer inserted into the pork reads 145°F.

4 Sprinkle the pork chops and apples with the bacon and the walnuts. Let the dish rest for 5 minutes before serving.

Crustless Ham and Broccoli Quiche

WITH THE EGGS, HAM, AND VEGGIES, there are enough hearty ingredients in this quiche to fill you up. Skipping the crust saves you time and turns this into a truly effortless weeknight dinner. Plus, you can heat up the leftovers for breakfast the next day for an energizing boost!

SERVES 8 ———————————————————————————

1 cup shredded Swiss cheese

1 cup part-skim shredded mozzarella cheese

2 tablespoons all-purpose flour

4 large eggs, lightly beaten

1½ cups milk

2 tablespoons chopped onion

¼ teaspoon kosher salt

⅛ teaspoon freshly ground black pepper

⅛ teaspoon dried thyme

⅛ teaspoon dried rosemary, crushed

½ cup diced fully cooked ham

½ cup chopped fresh broccoli

½ cup chopped red bell pepper

1 Preheat the oven to 350°F. Combine the cheeses with the flour in a small bowl, and set the bowl aside. In a large bowl, combine the eggs, milk, onion, and seasonings. Stir in the ham, broccoli, pepper, and cheese mixture, and mix until well combined.

2 Pour the mixture evenly into a 12-inch copper pan. Bake for 55-60 minutes, or until the eggs are set. Let the dish stand 10 minutes before serving.

Homestyle Pork Stew

DON'T BE FOOLED BY THE SLEW OF INGREDIENTS listed below—the flavors may be complex, but this recipe puts the "simple" in simply delicious. Make it for guests, and they'll think you're a gourmet cook! This is also one of those wonderful rainy-day dinners that warms you up from the inside out.

SERVES 6-8

¼ cup all-purpose flour

2½ teaspoons kosher salt, divided, plus extra, to taste

1½ teaspoons freshly ground black pepper, divided, plus extra, to taste

2½ pounds boneless pork roast, cubed

3 tablespoons extra virgin olive oil

2 small leeks, white and green part thinly sliced

1 cup chopped shallots

4 large garlic cloves, minced

1 cup white wine

5 medium carrots, peeled and cut into small pieces

4 medium Yukon Gold potatoes, peeled and cut into 1-inch cubes

2 cups chicken stock

1 (14.5-ounce) can chopped tomatoes

2 tablespoons balsamic vinegar

2 bay leaves

1 teaspoon dried basil

1 teaspoon dried oregano

1 teaspoon dried thyme

10 ounces cremini mushrooms, halved

Chopped parsley, for garnish

Chopped green onions, for garnish

1   In a medium bowl, combine the flour, ½ teaspoon of the salt, and ½ teaspoon of the black pepper. Add the pork cubes and toss to coat the meat.

2   Add the olive oil to a deep square copper pan over medium-high heat. Add half of the coated pork in a loose, even layer on the bottom of the pan.

Brown both sides of the pork for 2-3 minutes each before removing the meat from the pan and setting it aside. Repeat this step with the remaining coated pork.

3   Add the leeks, shallots, and garlic to the pan and sauté the ingredients for 2-3 minutes, or until the leeks are

wilted. Add the wine and stir everything until well combined, making sure to scrape the pan as you stir.

4   Stir in the carrots, potatoes, chicken stock, tomatoes, vinegar, bay leaves, basil, oregano, thyme, the remaining 2 teaspoons of salt, and the remaining 1 teaspoon of pepper. Bring the liquid to a boil, and then reduce the heat to low and simmer the ingredients for 5 minutes.

5   Return the pork to the pan, cover the pan with a lid, and simmer the ingredients for 30–40 minutes. Add the mushrooms, and continue simmering everything for 10–15 minutes, or until the vegetables are tender. Add more salt and pepper, if desired. Garnish the dish with the chopped parsley and green onions, and serve.

Ham and Veggie Pot Pie

SOUTHERN STAPLES like cornbread, ham, and collard greens come together to create the ultimate comfort food. Frozen vegetables save time, but you're welcome to chop up some fresh ones instead. And if the sauce doesn't thicken to your liking, add extra flour a little bit at a time.

SERVES 8–10 ────────────────────────

CORNBREAD CRUST BATTER

1½ cups white cornmeal mix

½ cup all-purpose flour

1 teaspoon sugar

2 large eggs, lightly beaten

1½ cups buttermilk

....

POT PIE FILLING

2 tablespoons vegetable oil

4 cups chopped cooked ham

3 tablespoons all-purpose flour

3 cups chicken broth

1 (14-ounce) package frozen diced onion, bell pepper, and celery mix

1 (16-ounce) package frozen chopped collard greens

1 (15.8-ounce) can black-eyed peas, rinsed and drained

½ teaspoon red pepper flakes

TO MAKE THE CORNBREAD CRUST BATTER

Combine the first 3 ingredients before adding the eggs and buttermilk to the mixture. Stir the ingredients together until just moistened.

TO MAKE THE POT PIE FILLING

1   Preheat the oven to 425°F. Add the oil to a deep square copper pan over medium-high heat. Add the ham, and sauté for 5 minutes, or until the meat is lightly browned. Add the flour, and stir the ingredients constantly for 1 minute more. Gradually add the chicken broth, and stirring the ingredients for 3 minutes, or until the broth begins to thicken.

2   Bring the liquid to a boil, and add the onion, bell pepper, celery mix and the collard greens. Stir the ingredients for 15 minutes before adding the black-eyed peas and red pepper flakes.

TO ASSEMBLE

Spread the cornbread crust batter evenly over the hot pot pie filling. Bake the dish for 20–25 minutes, or until the cornbread is golden brown and set.

Creamy Pork Chops and Potatoes

A SIMPLE CAN OF CREAM-OF-MUSHROOM SOUP makes all the difference, turning ordinary pork chops into something creamy and satisfying. Picky eaters will love the savory flavor blanketing their everyday dinner favorites. And the best part is how quickly it all comes together!

SERVES 4

1 tablespoon unsalted butter

4 (7-ounce) pork loin chops, ½-inch thick

3 medium red potatoes, cut into small wedges

3 medium carrots, sliced ½-inch thick

1 medium onion, cut into small wedges

1 (10¾-ounce) can condensed cream of mushroom soup

¼ cup water

1   Heat the butter in a 12-inch pan over medium heat. Brown the pork chops for 2-3 minutes on each side. Remove the pork chops from the pan and set aside, but reserve the pan drippings.

2   In the same pan, sauté the vegetables in the drippings until lightly browned, about 2 minutes. In a small bowl, whisk together the soup and water, and then add this mixture to the pan. Bring the liquid to a boil. Last, reduce the heat, cover the pan with a lid, and simmer for 15-20 minutes, or until the vegetables are just tender.

3   Return the pork chops to the pan, cover the pan again with a lid, and cook the ingredients until a thermometer inserted into the pork reads 145°F. Remove the pan from the heat and let stand for 5 minutes before serving.

Pork with Wild Rice and Vegetables

THIS IS ONE OF THOSE MIRACULOUS ONE-POT MEALS that practically makes itself. This simple mixture of pork, rice, vegetables, and herbs cooks up in just 20 minutes, and by the time it hits the table, you have a fully balanced dinner your family will love. Just make sure to grab a quick-cooking rice blend that cooks in around 20 minutes.

SERVES 4

1 pound lean pork tenderloin, diced

8 ounces sliced mushrooms

1½ cups chicken broth, reduced-sodium

1 cup quick-cook long-grain wild rice blend, uncooked

1 tablespoon favorite dried herb blend

1½ cups frozen mixed vegetables, thawed

kosher salt, to taste

freshly ground black pepper, to taste

1 In a 12-inch copper pan, combine the pork, mushrooms, broth, rice, and herbs. Bring the liquid to a boil. Reduce the heat to low, cover the pan with a lid, and simmer the ingredients for 15 minutes.

2 Stir in the mixed vegetables and continue to cook everything for about 5 minutes, or until the rice has absorbed the liquid and is tender, and the pork is cooked through. Season the dish with salt and pepper, to taste, before serving.

Chicken and Ham with Rice

A warming rice dish with a little bit of everything, Chicken and Ham with Rice is an easy one-pot meal that can bring together some of the easiest-to-find ingredients around: hearty chicken, cooked ham, frozen peas, and bell peppers. If you don't like ham or it's not a part of your diet, feel free to omit it, or toss in a few extra veggies in the last step.

SERVES 6

1 teaspoon + 1 tablespoon olive oil, divided

1 pound boneless, skinless chicken breast, cubed

½ teaspoon kosher salt, plus more to taste

¼ teaspoon freshly ground black pepper, plus more to taste

1 small yellow onion, diced

½ cup chopped cooked ham

2 cloves garlic, minced

2½ cups low-sodium chicken broth

1 cup frozen peas, thawed

1 red bell pepper, seeded and diced

1½ cups uncooked jasmine rice, rinsed

2 green onions, sliced and white parts removed

3 Put 1 teaspoon of the olive oil in a 12-inch copper pan over medium-high heat. Add the chicken to the pan, and season with salt and pepper, to taste. Cook the chicken until no longer pink, about 6–8 minutes. Remove the chicken from the pan, and set it aside.

4 Heat the remaining 1 tablespoon of olive oil in the same pan. Stir in the onion and ham, and sauté them for 5–7 minutes. Add the garlic, and cook for 1 additional minute.

5 Stir in the chicken broth, peas, red bell pepper, rice, measured salt, and measured pepper to combine all of the ingredients. Reduce the heat, cover the pan with a lid, and simmer the ingredients for 15–20 minutes, or until the rice is cooked through. Stir in the cooked chicken and green onion until the ingredients are well combined, and serve.

Salmon Fried Rice

THIS ISN'T YOUR EVERYDAY FRIED RICE—it's better! Salmon and asparagus add a touch of elegance to what is truly a simple and healthy weeknight meal. Thaw frozen salmon ahead of time and choose a quick-cooking rice blend to speed things up. *(Note: Make sure you have the butter you need for your rice prep.)*

1 (18.8-ounce) package quick-cook long-grain wild rice blend, uncooked

¼ cup chopped hazelnuts or almonds

8 ounces fresh or frozen salmon fillet

1 tablespoon olive oil

12 ounces thin fresh asparagus, trimmed and cut into 2-inch lengths

8 ounces sliced fresh mushrooms

1 medium leek, halved lengthwise and sliced

¼ teaspoon kosher salt

¼ teaspoon freshly ground black pepper

1–2 tablespoons dry sherry (optional)

fresh dill weed, for garnish

lemon wedges, for serving

1   In a deep square copper pan, cook the rice according to the package directions, adding the nuts while the rice is simmering. Remove the contents from the pan, and set them aside.

2   Rinse the salmon, pat it dry, and cut it into 1-inch pieces. Add the oil to the copper pan over medium-high heat. Add the salmon, and stir occasionally as you cook the fish for about 4 minutes, or until it flakes easily. Remove the salmon from the pan, and set it aside.

3   Return the pan to medium-high heat, and add the asparagus, mushrooms, leeks, salt, and pepper. Cook the ingredients for about 4 minutes, or until the asparagus is tender-crisp. Stir in the cooked rice and sherry (optional), and continue to cook everything for 4 minutes more, or until heated through. Gently fold in the cooked salmon, before topping the dish with dill weed and serving with a side of lemon wedges.

Clambake with Corn and Potatoes

HOW DO YOU MAKE AN ENTIRE BEACH BARBECUE IN A SINGLE PAN?
Easily, when you have a deep square copper pan. A mixture of chorizo, shellfish, and vegetables topped with lager brings the taste of New England's shores straight to your table.

SERVES 4

1 teaspoon extra virgin olive oil

2 links chorizo, sliced

1 medium yellow onion, chopped

1 pound baby red potatoes, halved

2 ears corn, halved

30 mussels

15 littleneck clams

1 bottle lager beer

kosher salt and freshly ground black pepper

parsley and lemon wedges, for garnish

1 Add the oil to an 11-inch copper casserole pan over medium heat. Add the chorizo and onion, and cook the ingredients for 3-4 minutes, or until the onion is tender and the chorizo is heated through.

2 Add the potatoes, corn, and shellfish. Pour in the beer; stir the ingredients until well combined. Cover the pan with a lid, and cook for 15–20 min, or until all of the shellfish have opened (discard any that haven't). Season the dish with salt and pepper, to taste, and serve it garnished with parsley and lemon wedges.

Shellfish Paella

CALLING ALL SHELLFISH FANATICS! Traditional paella tends to focus on a single type of seafood, but this recipe packs in several. Just make sure to be selective about your mussels, discarding any with shells that are broken or that remain open after tapping. You want the freshest seafood you can get to make this dish shine.

SERVES 4

1 tablespoon extra-virgin olive oil

½ cup chopped onion

½ cup chopped red bell pepper

2 cloves garlic, minced

2 cups instant brown rice, uncooked

1 ⅓ cups reduced-sodium chicken broth

½ teaspoon dried thyme

¼ teaspoon kosher salt

¼ teaspoon freshly ground black pepper

1 large pinch saffron

½ pound shrimp, peeled and deveined

½ pound sea scallops

¼ pound baby squid, cut into ¼-inch rings

1 cup frozen green peas, thawed

1 pound mussels, scrubbed well

4 lemon wedges, for garnish

1 Add the oil to an 11-inch copper casserole pan over medium heat. Add the onion, bell pepper, and garlic, and cook the ingredients for about 3 minutes, stirring occasionally, until the vegetables are softened. Mix in the rice, broth, thyme, salt, pepper, and saffron, and bring the liquid to a boil. Cover the pan with a lid and cook the ingredients for 5 minutes.

2 Stir in the shrimp, scallops, squid, and peas. Next, place the mussels on top of the mixture in an even layer. Cover the pan again, and continue cooking everything for about 5 more minutes, or until the mussels have opened and the rice is tender.

3 Remove the pan from the heat and let rest, covered, for 5 minutes, or until most of the liquid has absorbed. Serve this dish with a side of lemon wedges.

Sausage and Shrimp Jambalaya

YOU DON'T NEED A FANCY PAN AND A CULINARY DEGREE to make this southern cousin of paella—all this recipe requires is a 12-inch copper pan with a lid and little bit of stirring. While fresh-caught shrimp still in the shell are the most flavorful, previously peeled and deveined shrimp are still delicious and will save you some prep time.

SERVES 8

2 tablespoons olive oil, divided

¾ pound medium shrimp, peeled and deveined

1 (12-ounce) package chicken sausage, sliced into ½-inch rounds

1 medium onion, finely chopped

½ cup chopped mixed bell peppers

2 cloves garlic, minced

1½ cups long-grain rice, uncooked

¼ teaspoon paprika

¼ teaspoon ground turmeric

1 (14.5-ounce) can diced tomatoes

2 (14.5-ounce) cans reduced-sodium chicken broth

kosher salt and freshly ground black pepper

1 cup frozen green peas, thawed

1   Add 1 tablespoon of the oil to a 12-inch pan over medium-high heat. Add the shrimp, and cook them until just pink, about 2 minutes per side. (Make sure not to overcook them.) Remove the shrimp from the pan and set them aside.

2   Add the remaining 1 tablespoon of oil and the sausage to the pan. Cook the meat over medium-high heat until the sausage starts to brown, about 2 minutes. Stir in the onion and peppers, and cook the ingredients for 3-4 minutes, or until translucent. Mix in the garlic and rice, and cook everything for an additional 1-2 minutes, or until the rice is translucent.

3   Stir in the paprika, turmeric, tomatoes, and broth, stirring the mixture frequently. Season the dish with salt and pepper, to taste.

4   Bring the liquid to a boil, then reduce the heat to a simmer. Cover the pan with a lid, and let the ingredients cook for 20–25 minutes, until the rice is tender and has absorbed most of the liquid. Stir in the peas and cook the dish for 1 minute more. Return cooked shrimp to the pan, and serve immediately.

New England Clam Chowder

SOME NIGHTS ARE JUST SOUP NIGHTS. With clams, potatoes, bacon, and cream, this is certainly a meal unto itself. But if you're looking for that little something extra, try serving it with homemade garlic bread.

SERVES 5

4 center-cut bacon strips, sliced into small strips width-wise

2 celery ribs, chopped

1 large onion, chopped

1 garlic clove, minced

3 small potatoes, peeled and cubed

1 cup water

1 (8-ounce) bottle clam juice

3 teaspoons reduced-sodium chicken bouillon granules

¼ teaspoon white pepper

¼ teaspoon dried thyme

⅓ cup all-purpose flour

2 cups fat-free half-and-half, divided

2 (6.5-ounce) cans chopped clams, undrained

1 In a deep square copper pan, cook the bacon over medium heat until it is crisp., Transfer the bacon to paper towels to drain, reserving the drippings in the pan.

2 Sauté the celery and onion in the bacon drippings until the vegetables are tender. Add the garlic, and cook the ingredients for 1 more minute, until fragrant. Stir in the potatoes, water, clam juice, bouillon, white pepper, and thyme. Bring the liquid to a boil, then reduce the heat, and simmer the dish, uncovered, for 15–20 minutes, or until the potatoes are tender.

3 In a small bowl, mix together the flour and 1 cup of the half-and-half until the consistency is smooth. Slowly stir the flour mixture into the pan contents. Bring the liquid to a boil, then stir for 1–2 minutes until the soup has thickened.

4 Stir in the clams, the remaining half-and-half, and the bacon, and heat all of the ingredients through before serving hot.

Turkey Tetrazzini Casserole

THIS RECIPE WORKS WONDERS with either leftover turkey or leftover chicken, but you can also make it using a freshly bought rotisserie chicken. It hits all the classic comfort food high notes—pasta, cheese, meat, and bread—and creates a beautiful presentation fit for serving to guests.

SERVES 6

1 tablespoon unsalted butter

½ cup finely chopped onion

⅓ cup finely chopped celery

½ teaspoon kosher salt

½ teaspoon freshly ground black pepper

¾ cup diced carrot

8 ounces sliced mushrooms (optional)

½ cup all-purpose flour

½ cup white wine

4 cups chicken broth

1 cup Parmesan cheese, divided

4 ounces light cream cheese

¾ cup frozen peas

2 cups cooked and shredded turkey meat

8 ounces thin spaghetti, uncooked

½ cup breadcrumbs or panko

1   Preheat the oven to 350°F. Melt the butter in an 11-inch copper casserole pan over medium heat. Add the onion, celery, salt, pepper, carrots, and mushrooms, and sauté until the vegetables are tender. Stir in the flour until all of the vegetables are coated. Add the wine, and stir quickly until the flour absorbs all of the liquid. Gradually add the broth, stirring constantly.

2   Bring the liquid to a boil, then reduce the heat and simmer for 5 minutes, stirring the ingredients frequently. Remove the pan from the heat, and add ½ cup of the Parmesan cheese and all of the cream cheese, stirring until both cheeses melt. Mix in the peas, turkey, and pasta until the ingredients are well combined.

3   In a small bowl, combine the breadcrumbs with the remaining ½ cup of Parmesan cheese. Evenly dust the casserole with the breadcrumb and cheese mixture, then transfer the pan to the oven, and bake for 30 minutes, or until lightly browned. Let the dish stand for 15 minutes before serving.

Turkey and Wild Rice Casserole

SIT BACK AND RELAX while your dinner practically makes itself! Cream of mushroom soup makes quick work of adding depth to this dish, so all you have to do is pour everything into a pan and pop it in the oven. Not in the mood for turkey? Replace the protein with cooked chicken or ham.

SERVES 6

2 cups cooked and chopped turkey

2¼ cups boiling water

⅓ cup milk

¼ cup chopped onion

1 pound button mushrooms

1 (10¾-ounce) can condensed cream of mushroom soup

1 (6-ounce) package seasoned long-grain wild rice blend, uncooked

fresh parsley, for garnish

1 Heat the oven to 350°F. In an 11-inch copper casserole pan, mix together all of the ingredients, including the seasoning packet from the rice mix.

2 Cover with a lid and bake for 45–50 minutes or until the rice is tender. Uncover the pan and bake for 10–15 more minutes, or until the liquid is absorbed. Serve with parsley for a garnish.

Pasta Primavera

THIS RECIPE IS GREAT FOR NIGHTS when you want a pasta that's satisfying but not heavy. A large helping of healthy green vegetables and just a splash of cream make this delicious dish a little less guilty of a pleasure. If you prefer mushrooms or other vegetables to snow peas, feel free to sub them in.

SERVES: 4-6

4 cups low-sodium vegetable broth

8 ounces penne, uncooked

1 small onion, halved and sliced thin

2 cups broccoli florets

1½ pounds green beans

1 cup snow peas

4 large cloves garlic, minced

1 teaspoon kosher salt, plus extra for taste

½ teaspoon freshly ground black pepper, plus extra for taste

2 tablespoons olive oil

½ cup chopped fresh parsley

¼ cup heavy whipping cream

2 tablespoons grated Parmesan cheese, plus extra for serving

2 teaspoons lemon zest

¼ teaspoon chives, for serving

1   In a deep copper pan over high heat, mix together the broth, pasta, onion, broccoli, green bean, snow peas, garlic, salt, and pepper. Drizzle the olive oil over the top of the ingredients. Bring the liquid to a boil, and cook for 7 minutes, using tongs to toss frequently.

2   Add the parsley, heavy whipping cream, Parmesan, and lemon zest to the pan, and continue tossing the ingredients for 1-2 more minutes, or until the pasta and veggies appear tender. Remove the pan from the heat.

3   Let the pasta sit for a couple of minutes to cool while the sauce thickens. Season with extra salt or pepper to taste. Garnish the dish with chives and extra Parmesan cheese before serving.

Eggplant Parmesan Pasta

WHY SERVE EGGPLANT PARM WITH A SIDE OF PASTA when you can combine the two into something even better? This flavor-packed family favorite serves up plenty of veggies, so there's no need to feel guilty about a little pasta and cheese. But if you like, swap out regular pasta for a healthier whole-grain version.

SERVES 4–6

2½ tablespoons olive oil

1 medium onion, chopped

3 large cloves garlic, minced

2 to 2¼ pounds eggplant, cubed

½ teaspoon kosher salt

¼ to ½ teaspoon red pepper flakes

1 (5-ounce) bag fresh baby spinach leaves

1 (14.5-ounce) can fire-roasted diced tomatoes

1 (8-ounce) can tomato sauce

1½ cups low-sodium vegetable broth

8 ounces linguine, uncooked

1¼ cups part-skim shredded mozzarella cheese

¼ cup shredded Parmesan cheese

fresh parsley, for garnish

1   Add the olive oil to a deep square copper pan over medium heat. Add the onion, and cook it for about 2 minutes, or until tender. Add the garlic, and cook it for 30 seconds, or until aromatic. Stir in the eggplant, salt, and red pepper flakes, cooking for 7–8 minutes, or until the eggplant is tender. Stir in the spinach and cook it until wilted. Transfer all the veggies to a medium bowl and set it aside.

2   In the same pan, add the diced tomatoes, tomato sauce, broth, and pasta, and stir the ingredients until well combined. Bring the liquid to a boil, then reduce the heat to medium-low, cover the pan with a lid, and simmer the ingredients for about 11–13 minutes, stirring occasionally (and more frequently toward the end of the cooking time), until the pasta is al dente and almost all of the liquid has absorbed.

3 Reduce the heat to low, and stir in
the vegetable mixture. Top evenly with
the mozzarella and Parmesan cheeses,
then cover the pan again, and continue
to cook for 3–5 minutes, or until the

cheese has melted. Remove the pan from
heat, and let the pasta rest for 5 minutes.
Garnish with fresh parsley, and season
with additional salt and pepper flakes, to
taste, before serving.

Lemon Pepper Chicken Risotto

DON'T BE AFRAID TO TRY THIS ONE—risotto is just a fancy word for creamy rice. Add a little Parmesan, garlic, and lemon-pepper chicken to the mix, and you have one amazing one-pot meal your guests will love. *(Note: You can find lemon pepper seasoning in the spice aisle at any grocery store.)*

½ tablespoon olive oil

2 pounds chicken thighs, bone-in with skin

2-3 tablespoons lemon pepper seasoning

2 tablespoons unsalted butter

4 garlic cloves, minced

1 onion, finely diced

1½ cups risotto rice (arborio)

½ cup white wine

4 cups chicken broth

1¾ cup milk, divided

½ teaspoon kosher salt

freshly ground black pepper, to taste

1 cup freshly Parmesan cheese, grated

2 tablespoons unsalted butter

---

1   Preheat the oven to 350°F. Add the olive oil to a 12-inch copper pan over medium heat. While the oil heats, coat the chicken with lemon pepper seasoning before placing the chicken in the pan, skin-side down. Cook the meat for 3 minutes, then turn the heat up to a medium-high setting, and cook the chicken for another 2 minutes, or until browned. Flip the meat and continue cooking it for 3 more minutes. Transfer the chicken to a plate, and wipe out the pan.

2   Return the pan to medium-high heat, and add butter. When melted, add the garlic and onion, and cook for 2 minutes or until the onion softens.

3   Stir in the rice until the grains become translucent. Add the wine, and cook for 1–2 minutes, or until the liquid is mostly absorbed. Stir in the chicken broth, 1 cup of the milk, the salt, and the pepper, and lower the heat to a simmer. Return the chicken to the pan, placing it on top of the rice and pouring the juices over the top.

4 Bake, covered with a lid, for 20 minutes, then remove the lid and return the pan to the oven for another 10 minutes, or until the rice is firm and the chicken is crispy (you don't want mushy rice!). Momentarily remove the chicken from the rice. Stir in the Parmesan cheese, butter, and the remaining ¾ cup milk, warmed, to create the creamy risotto. Return the chicken to the pan, and serve.

Index